BEYOND SCHMUTZ: THE CURSES, SLANG, AND STREET LINGO
YOU NEED TO KNOW WHEN YOU SPEAK DEUTSCH

TALK DIRTY
GERMAN

ALEXIS MUNIER & KARIN EBERHARDT

Adamsmedia

Avon, Massachusetts

Published by
Adams Media, a divison of F+W Media, Inc.
57 Littlefield Street, Avon, MA 02322
www.adamsmedia.com

ISBN 10: 1-60550-653-2
ISBN 13: 978-1-60550-653-1

Printed in the United States of America.

J I H G F E D C B A

Library of Congress Cataloging-in-Publication Data
is available from the publisher.

This publication is designed to provide accurate and authoritative information with regard to the subject matter covered. It is sold with the understanding that the publisher is not engaged in rendering legal, accounting, or
other professional advice. If legal advice or other expert assistance is required, the services of a competent professional person should be sought.
    —From a *Declaration of Principles* jointly adopted by a Committee of the
American Bar Association and a Committee of Publishers and Associations

Many of the designations used by manufacturers and sellers to distinguish
their product are claimed as trademarks. Where those designations appear
in this book and Adams Media was aware of a trademark claim, the designations have been printed with initial capital letters.

Interior illustrations ©iStockphoto.com/Matt Knannlein.

This book is available at quantity discounts for bulk purchases.
For information, please call 1-800-289-0963.

Contents

GERMAN
READER
ADVISORY

To my husband Matt,
who always has the right words for me.
—Karin Eberhardt

To my husband Emmanuel,
who should watch his words more carefully.
—Alexis Munier

Acknowledgments

A heartfelt thank you to Emmanuel Tichelli, David Nuñez, Jacques B., Matt Burcaw, Irmgard Eberhardt, Silke and Martin Eichholz, Doris Altmann, Anja Uske, and James Sylvester, who all took the time to get down and dirty for this book.

And one last thanks to our publisher, Adams Media, and its supportive team, including Paula Munier, Matthew Glazer, Tammi Reichel, and Denise Wallace.

FIRST CLASS

INTRODUCTION

Ah *Deutsch*—while French may be considered the language of love and Spanish deemed by many the future of the United States, this steadfast *Sprache* has its merits as well. Not just a one-trick pony, *Deutsch* has been influencing Europe for centuries. Used in one form or another in Germany, Switzerland, Austria, Liechtenstein, Luxembourg, and in parts of Denmark, France, Belgium, and Italy, it is also the most widely spoken second language in the majority of Eastern Europe.

Some may stereotype German as harsh and unpleasant, but those lucky enough to know better are acutely aware of its logical, yet oddly romantic nature. After all, the language gave birth to romanticism, inspiring poetic and musical genius in greats like Goethe, Heine, and Brahms. Then again, it also shaped the hearts and minds of Milli Vanilli and the Governator.

But how to reconcile traditional *Hochdeutsch* with the current state of the German tongue? Germany's own regional dialects and incomprehensible derivatives in Switzerland and Austria may leave you wondering if you have had one too many pints of *Hefeweizen* or are just a plain old *Dummkopf*. No fear—*Talk Dirty: German* is here to give you a basic introduction into the netherworlds (and nether regions) of the true *Jargon* you're likely to hear in the German-speaking world. Whether seducing a *Mädchen* in München or a *Kerl* in Köln, your rate of success can only increase with this gritty linguistic guide.

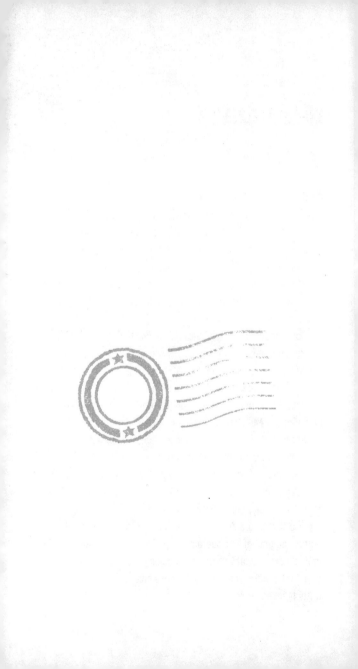

CHAPTER ONE

Man spricht kein Deutsch:
What's That Strange Language?

Germany as a country did not exist until 1871, so it's understandable that a unified German language struggled before that time. Made up of various *Länder*, Germany has long been home to a variety of regional dialects. The first steps toward cementing a German language were taken by Martin Luther. Not Dr. King, but his older, whiter, German namesake. In both his New and Old Testament translations (1521 and 1534), Martin Luther used *Sächsiche*, spoken in the region of Saxony, which was the most widely understood dialect at that time. To help the good book reach as many *Sündere*, sinners, as possible, copies originally had a long list of vocabulary words that were translated into different regional dialects. Even today, German pronunciation varies from region to region—which is why a hustler from Hamburg might have difficulties understanding what those beer-guzzling Bavarians are babbling about at Oktoberfest.

Did you know that Goldilocks and Little Red Riding Hood also shared an important role in the creation of modern German? Well,

1

not exactly, but the Brothers Grimm, famously associated with fairy tales, also published a dictionary, which was the most complete guide to German available. Then, in the twentieth century, the Duden Handbook took over as the respected guardian of the German language. More recently, a controversial spelling reform was introduced in the mid-1990s. The controversy focused on whether a language is an unmalleable cultural identity or rather a living, breathing, and constantly changing tool for communication. After a decade of bickering fueled by peppermint *Schnapps* and *Lëbkuchen*, parliament finally approved the reform. While the new spelling rules are easier for international use, the authors bemoan the loss of the cute little umlauts (ö,ä,ü) and the superbly statuesque ess-laut (ß).

Foreign Influences in German

German is by no means pure; over the years it has been influenced by many different languages, including French, Latin, Greek, and most recently English and Turkish.

French vs English in German

A very common phrase still in use is: *Wie Gott in Frankreich leben*, literally "to live like God in France," or to live in the lap of luxury. Since when did the French have things so good, you may ask yourself. If that's the case, be sure to check out *Talk Dirty: French* for all the answers.

While the French once had a strong influence on the Germans, today French is at best *passé* –if not "out" completely. German used to be full of French expressions (such as the idiom *Wie Gott in Frankreich leben*), but this was before ridiculous French rockers like Johnny Hallyday and Claude François destroyed Germany's faith in their neighboring nation. Thankfully, the Germans came to their senses when seduced by the likes of Britney Spears and Coca-Cola. But when God still lived in France, German *savoir vivre* hit a high note; today's American-influenced *Lifestyle* falls a bit flat. *Rendez-vous* have been replaced by the *Date*, and caviar and champagne *Fêten* have given way to the less glamorous *Pizza Party*.

Denglisch

Denglisch, a combination of the words *Deutsch* and *Englisch*, is a form of slang currently in use in all of the German-speaking world. It mixes German and English willy-nilly, making for strange syntax and grammar. While France has a high commission to develop new French words to replace imported American terms, Germany has no such body . . . yet.

Germanization of English Words

As it has no set of grammar rules, *Denglisch* verbs run the gamut from traditional German-type conjugations to decidedly American ones (note the unusual past tense and its two variations):

downloaden
to download
Ich habe letzte Woche einen kostenlosen Pornofilm gedownloaded, aber meine Frau hat ihn gelöscht.
I downloaded a free porno last week but my wife deleted it.

chillen
to chill
Halt einfach den Mund und chille, Mann!
Just shut up and chill, man!

More on Grammar

Denglisch also features English usage that is incorrect in German. As an example, some prepositions have changed to reflect their English equivalents:

TBG   Im Jahre 1990 fiel die Berliner Mauer.
DG   In 1990 fiel die Berliner Mauer.

The Berlin Wall fell in 1990.

Mixed Bag

A sentence in *Denglisch* can often be be created simply by stringing English and German words together:

TBG   Mein toller Liebhaber entwirft für seine Firma Klei-
**   dung für Alleinstehende und leitet nebenbei die**
**   Firmenmannschaft.**
DG   Mein cooler Lover designt für seine Firma Outfits
**   für Singles und managt nebenbei das Firmenteam.**

My cool lover designs outfits for singles for his company and also manages the company team.

TBG   Ich habe keine Ahnung.
DG   I have keine Idee.

I have no idea.

TBG   Ich brauche neue Kleidung, lass uns einkaufen
**   gehen.**
DG   Ich brauche neue Outfits, lass uns shoppen gehen.

I need new clothes; let's go shopping.

Often, *Denglisch* speakers will substitute a German word with the English equivalent:

TBG   **Hey, Klaus ist heute so gut gekleidet, ich wette er hat später eine Verabredung.**

DG   **Hey, Klaus ist heute so dressed-up, ich wette er hat später ein Date.**

Hey, Klaus is so dressed-up today, I bet he has a date later.

TBG   **Der Verkaufsschlager war einfach unglaublich.**

DG   **Der Bestseller war einfach unbelievable.**

The bestseller was simply unbelievable.

TBG   **Der Kundin wurde eine gründliche Veränderung und ein neues Aussehen versprochen.**

DG   **Der Kundin wurde ein komplettes Make-over und ein neuer Look versprochen.**

The customer was promised a complete makeover and a new look.

Perhaps the fall of the dollar and the lessoning of U.S. influence in the world will lead to a reduction of English words in the German business sphere. But today English sneaks its way into almost all commercial products and services.

While using *Deutsche Telekom*, don't forget that there are *Sunshine* and *Moonshine-Tarife*. You will pay more for the sunshine. Instead, you may want to make a *City Call* which is cheaper than long distance.

If you have a letter to mail, you'll go to the *Deutsche Post*, where you can do some *One Stop Shopping*, and one of your stops will be at the *Postage Point* to get your stamps.

When traveling by train, make sure you find the *Service Points* in the Bahnhof. You can purchase a *City Express Ticket* and then go to a *Meeting Point* or relax in a *DB* (Deutsche Bahn)-*Lounge* while waiting for your ICE (*InterCityExpress*).

After you arrive at your destination, you may want to get a *Coffee-to-go* (used instead of the German *Kaffee zum Mitnehmen*). But if you have enough time you can find a bar that has a *Happy Hour* (rather than the correct *Blaue Stunde*) or a restaurant with an *All-You-Can-Eat Buffet*.

To do all of the aforementioned things you'll need some money, so you better head to the bank and talk to your *Account-Betreuer*.

Here is a list of German slang words that sound English but don't quite mean what you might think they should:

German Word	Meaning
Baracke, f.	hut, shed, run-down house
Billion, f.	trillion
Body-Bag, f.	backpack
Chef, m.	boss
down/uploaden	to down/upload
Dressman, m.	male model
Evergreen, m.	golden oldie
Handy, n.	mobile phone
jobben	to do short-term work, to have a summer job
mobbing	bullying
Oldtimer, m.	vintage or classic car, or aircraft
Präservativ, n.	condom

German Word	Meaning
Shooting, n.	photo shoot
Showmaster, m.	TV show host
Slip, m.	briefs, panties
Smoking, m.	tuxedo, dinner jacket
Spleen, m.	tic
String, m.	thong
trampen	hitchhiking

Kanak Sprak: Turkish Takeover Is Not Limited to Kebabs Alone

Kanak Sprak is a German ethnolect created by Turkish youth in the late 1980s. This 'sociolect' is named for the book *Kanak Sprak* (1995) by German-Turkish author Feridun Zaimoglu who introduced readers to a unique combination of German and Turkish slang. Its name comes from the Turkish word *Kanake*, which was originally an insult for Turks, and *Sprach*, talk. Minorities and immigrants now embrace the word *Kanake*, comparable to some African Americans using the word "niggah."

Kanak Sprak is gaining in popularity, especially among urban youth, who use it to express mostly sex terms, greetings, insults, and feelings.

Sometimes *Kanak Sprak* is just a simple Turkish word that takes the place of a German one:

lan, Turkey
man/dude
Tam tschuki lan! (from the Turkish *Tamam cok iyi lan!*)
Pretty damn cool, man!

Often, though, *Kanak Sprak* has its own grammar and spelling rules, which are nearly impossible to predict. Prepositions and articles are seldom used, and schwas (the final 'e'), especially in first-person conjugations, are dropped:

TBG   **Ich gehe zum Bahnhof.**
DG   **Isch geh Bahnhof.**

I'm going to the train station.

Other times, *Kanak Sprak* respells German words the way they sound when pronounced. Often, *oda was* (TBG *oder was)*, "or what," is added at the end of a phrase:

TBG   **Hast Du Probleme? Oder bist Du ein Spinner?**
DG   **Was hast du für Problem? Bissu Spinna oda was?**

You gotta problem? Are you stupid or what?

Austrian and Swiss German—The Other Two German Languages

When you arrive in Switzerland or Austria, you might be in for a shock if you hope to speak your high school German here. Although *Hochdeutsch* appears in all written forms of the language (i.e. newspapers, signs, menus) you may not grasp what these folks in *Lederhosen* are saying, even if your German is pretty good. Don't worry, even Germans have a hard time understanding the Austrians and the Swiss. When Swiss or Austrians speak in their native dialect, the grammar, intonation, and even the vocabulary are different. No wonder Germans watch Swiss or Austrians movies either dubbed or with subtitles. Because these dialects are not slang unto themselves, we won't go into Swiss and Austrian here. We can, however, give you just a few examples of true Alpine lingo:

Piefke, m., Austria
Kraut, Heini, Jerry
Piefke, Spaghettifresser und Schlitzauge sind alles doofe Schimpfwörter für Leute eines anderen Landes.
Piefke, guinea, and chink are all stupid insults and derogatory terms for people from other countries.

Austrians use the word Piefke *as a disparaging term for a German, somewhat like the Mexican use of gringo for an American. Even in Hochdeutsch, a* Piefke *is a "pompous idiot," so it is not a word to be used lightly. Ein kleiner Piefke is "a little pipsqueak."*

Gopfertami!, Switzerland (Bernese)
Goddamn it!, lit. God damn me!
"Gopfertami!" rief sie aus.
"Goddamn it!" she cried.

Schaafsekku, m., Switzerland
fucking moron, lit. sheep's cock
Haut dini klappe, du huere Schaafsekku!
Shut your hole, you fucking moron!

CHAPTER TWO

Willkommen:

Getting Off on the Right Foot

About a quarter of all citizens of the United States, around 70 million, claim at least partial German ancestry. But oddly enough, it was an Irishman who endeared the United States to Germany once again in the mid-1960s. When President John F. Kennedy made his famous speech in West Berlin, he resounded, "*Ich bin ein Berliner.*" If only his speechwriter had known that a *Berliner* is also what the city's famous doughnuts are called. President Kennedy should have simply stated: "*Ich bin Berliner.*"

Nowadays, introducing yourself presents another problem . . . Germans may find you pretentious or rude when claiming to be *Amerikaner*. They'll immediately point out that America is a actually two separate continents, north and south, and not a country. Rather than getting offended, we suggest just chuckling and reminding them that *Amerikaner* is the German word for a U.S. citizen. When they come up with a new term, you'll be happy to use it.

But perhaps the most important thing to watch when introducing yourself in Germany is your choice of formal or informal language.

DU and SIE:

Many languages have formal and informal forms of address, but the Germans are, of course, extremely gründlich, "strict," along those lines. Always use the formal Sie unless your conversation partner suggests to use the informal du. In business situations, men and women are always referred to as Herr and Frau.

The formal form of address is not just limited to business settings. Even after twenty years, next-door neighbors might still siezen each other. Although etiquette is changing with the younger folks, a nice tradition prevails: In order to officially drop the Sie and start using the informal du, two people toast each other (of course with beer) and close the pact to call each other du, and by their first names.

Meet the Family

meine Alten, pl

my parents; lit. my old ones

Meine Alten gehen mir derzeit ganz schön auf den Sack.

My parents are really getting on my nerves these days.

Kohlenbeschaffer, pl

parents; lit. coal diggers

Horst kann nicht mit uns ins Kino kommen. Seine Kohlenbeschaffer sind total geizig.

Horst can't come with us to the movies. His parents are totally stingy.

nicht von schlechten Eltern sein
to be not half bad; lit. not from bad parents
Sein Englisch ist nicht von schlechten Eltern.
His English isn't half bad.

Hotel Mama, n.
home; lit. Hotel Mother
Er wohnt noch immer im Hotel Mama, weil's billiger und bequemer ist.
He's still living at home because it is cheaper and easier.

Muttersöhnchen, n.
mama's boy, lit. mother's little son
Wie kannst du nur mit Christian gehen? Der ist das totale Muttersöhnchen.
How can you date Christian? He's a total mama's boy.

Kniebeißer, pl.
rugrats; lit. knee biters
Dirk: "Gestern wollte sich doch glatt so ein Kniebeißer an der Kinokasse vordrängeln." Holger: "Was die sich rausnehmen."
Dirk: "Yesterday this little rugrat tried to jump the line at the movies." Holger: "The nerve."

Bälger, pl.
kids
Die Bälger heutzutage haben überhaupt keinen Respekt mehr vor Erwachsenen.
Kids today have no respect for their elders anymore.

Plagen, pl.
children; lit. troubles
"Schau doch mal nach, was die Plagen machen."
"Can you check what the children are up to?"

Nesthäkchen, n.
baby of the family, nestling
Sonja ist das Netshäkchen in der Familie und wird von allen verwöhnt.
Sonja is the baby of the family and is spoiled by everyone.

Sohnemann, m.
junior; lit. son-man
Tag, Frau Meier, wie geht's dem Sohnemann?
Hello Ms. Meier, how's your son?

Halbstarken, pl.
adolescent; lit. half-strongs
Du führst dich auf wie ein Halbstarker. Werd mal erwachsen.
You are acting like a real adolescent. Grow up.

Krampfadergeschwader, n.
senior citizens; lit. varicose vein brigade
Da hat mir doch glatt jemand vom Krampfadergeschwader erzählen wollen, ich könnte hier nicht rauchen.
One of these old farts tried to tell me I couldn't smoke here.

grufties, pl.
old people; lit. people living in a vault
Manche Grufties haben noch ganz gute Ideen.
Some old people still come up with good ideas.

Angetrauten, pl.
the in-laws
Ich komme gut mit meinen Angetrauten klar.
I get along fine with my in-laws.

Lesterschwein, n.

sister, actually 'Schwesterlein' jumbled

Klaus, darf ich vorstellen: mein Lesterschwein.

Klaus, meet my sister.

Lebensabschnittsgefährte, m.;
Lebensabschnittsgefährtin, f.

partner; lit. stage-of-life partner

Sie ist seit zwei Jahren meine Lebensabschnittsgefährtin.

She's been my partner for two years now.

In today's world, people (yes, even Germans) tend to change their partners as often as they change their underwear. A Lebensabschnittsgefährte/in *is a long-term* Partner *who accompanies one for just a certain stage of one's life. Hence, should your* Leben *evolve, so might your choice of loved one.*

Gardinenpredigt halten, f.

to chew someone out; lit. to give a curtain sermon

Nachdem mein Vater mich beim Rauchen erwischte, hat er mir eine Gardinenpredigt gehalten.

After my father caught me smoking, he chewed me out.

Putzfimmel, m.

clean freak; lit. to have a mania for cleaning

Meine Frau zu Hause hat den Putzfimmel, da ist nichts und niemand vor ihr sicher.

My wife is such a clean freak; nothing or nobody can stand in her way.

Drachenfutter, n.
peace offerings or make-up gifts; lit. dragon fodder
Rosen und Pralinen sind geeignetes Drachenfutter.
Roses and chocolates are good make-up gifts.

Ex, m./f.
ex-partner
Mein Ex hat mich gestern angerufen.
My ex called me yesterday.

Beziehungskiste, f.
friendship/relationship; lit. relationship box
In ihrer Beziehungskiste krachte es gewaltig!
They had a serious relationship crisis!

Macker, m.
boyfriend, originally derived from *Macher*=maker, doer
Das ist ihr neuer Macker.
That's her new boyfriend.

Scheich, m.
boyfriend; lit. sheik
Carols Scheich ist voll der Angeber.
Carol's boyfriend is a real showoff.

Ische, f.
girlfriend; lit. gal
Die Ische vom Stefan könnte mir auch gefallen.
I wouldn't say no to Stefan's girlfriend.

Auserkorene, f.
girlfriend, fiancée; lit. the chosen one
Hast Du schon die Auserkorene von deinem Bruder kennengelernt?
Have you met your brother's girlfriend yet?

15

Tussi, f.
chick, woman
Schau dir mal die Tussi an!
Check out this chick!

Frauenzimmer, n.
bitch
Kerstin ist ein ganz gemeines Frauenzimmer.
Kerstin is a mean bitch.

Weib, n.
broad
Weiber können mir gestohlen bleiben. Die machen nix als Kopfschmerzen.
I'm fed up with broads. They cause nothing but headaches.

Zicke, f.
bitch; lit. nanny goat
Die Brigitte kann 'ne ganz große Zicke sein. Sei bloß vorsichtig.
Brigitte can be a real bitch sometimes. Watch out.

Zickenstall, m.
ladies' room; lit. nanny goats' stable
Warum ist die Schlange vorm Zickenstall immer drei Mal so lang wie bei den Männern?
Why is the line to the ladies room always three times as long as the men's line?

Zickenalarm, m.
bitch alert; lit. nanny goat alert
Zickenalarm—die Klara und die Andrea haben sich wieder in die Haare gekriegt.
Bitch alert—Klara and Andrea are locking horns again.

16

Typ, m.
guy
Der Typ dort starrt dich schon die ganze Zeit an.
The guy over there was checking you out the entire time.

Heini, m.
guy, actually a nickname for the name Heinrich
Ulf: "Wo sind denn hier die Toiletten? "
Tim: "Keine Ahnung, frag doch mal den Heini dort am Infor-mationsstand. "
Ulf: "You know where the bathrooms are?"
Tim: "No idea. Go ask the guy at customer service."

Clique, f.
buddies, clique
Am Wochenende mache ich immer was mit meiner Clique.
On the weekends I always hang out with my buddies.

MOF, m.
loner, actually an acronym for *Mensch ohne Freunde*, or person with no friends
Dieter is voll der MOF. Den hab ich noch nie auf 'ner Party gesehen.
Dieter is a complete loner. I've never seen him at a party.

Hallöchen
Hi
Hallöchen. Lange nicht gesehen.
Hi. I haven't seen you in a while.

Tschüss
Bye
Tschüss—mach's gut!
Bye, take care!

Ciao
bye (but also used for 'hello')
Ciao. Bis bald.
Bye. See ya.

paletti
ok
Alles paletti bei dir?
Everything ok with you?

Was ist los?
What's up?
He, was ist los mit dir, Mann?
Hey, what's up, man?

CHAPTER THREE

Dummkopf:

Smart, Stupid, or Just Plain Nuts

One of the most famous Germans of all time is undeniably Albert Einstein. Germans like to take credit for his genius and consider themselves a truly intelligent people, ignoring the fact that his smartest move was to leave Germany for Switzerland and later the United States. Moving on, Germany is also known for its bevy of beautiful supermodels, including Claudia Schiffer and Heidi Klum. We can't vouch for their IQs, but these lovely ladies managed to make million-dollar careers of their bodies (and who says Germans are pudgy?). Last but not least, we have the crazy German-spea-kers . . . guys like Sigmund Freud, the father of psychoanalysis. While most shrinks treat the loonies for a living, Freud may have been one himself. His theory of penis envy, which states that all women long for a penis whether they realize it or not, is perhaps the most well-known. Frankly, in our book he was a nutter; we all know that you don't need a penis to rule the world. Just ask Hillary Clinton, who may feel that Barack Obama suffers from this condition himself . . . many Germans feel that if he had any balls, he would've chosen her as his running mate.

Idiot, m.

jerk

Was bildest du dir eigentlich ein, du Idiot?

Who do you think you are, jerk?

dummschwallen

to talk nonsense/to talk out of one's ass

Hör auf dummzuschwallen!

Stop talking out of your ass!

Dumpfbacke, f.

dummy/idiot/bore; lit. hollow cheeks

Dein Freund sieht ja nett aus, aber er ist eine richtige Dumpfbacke.

Your boyfriend looks cute, but he's a real dummy.

Ödbacke, f.

bore; lit. bleak or dreary cheeks

Den ganzen Abend lang hat Arnold nur über sein Auto gesprochen, was für eine Ödbacke.

All evening long, Arnold just talked about his car. What a bore!

Dachschaden haben

to be crazy; lit. to have a broken roof

Meine Eltern haben einen Dachschaden wenn sie glauben, ich komme schon um 22 Uhr heim.

My parents must be crazy if they think I'll come home at 10 p.m.

Riß in der Schüssel haben

to be crazy; lit. to have a crack in the bowl

Wie kannst du so mit mir reden? Hast du'n Riss in der Schüssel, oder was?

How can you talk to me like that? Are you crazy, or what?

labern

to talk bullshit; to blabber

Laber doch keinen Mist. Ihr habt total geflirtet.

Stop talking bullshit. You guys were totally flirting.

Labern *can also just refer to talking endlessly, droning on, blabbering, without the negative connotation of talking bullshit.*

Labersack, m.

blabbermouth; lit. babble–bag

Michael ist ein Labersack, der erzählt alles weiter.

Michael is such a blabbermouth; he tells everything to everyone.

jemandem einen Blumenkohl ans Ohr quatschen

to talk/chew someone's ear off; lit. to talk a cauliflower onto someone's ear

Mach nicht den Fehler David über Sex zu fragen; er wird dir einen Blumenkohl ans Ohr quatschen.

Don't make the mistake of asking David about sex; he'll chew your ear off.

jemandem sülzen

to go on and on to someone

Alexandra hat mit ihren Freundinnen total gesülzt aber hat die ganze Nacht kein Wort zu mir gesagt.

Alexandra went on and on to her friends but didn't say a word to me all night.

Pappnase, f.

joke, stupid person; lit. fake nose

21

Der Typ ist so doof—voll die Pappnase.
This guy is so stupid—he's a joke.

abgedreht
nuts; lit. turned away or turned off
Der Typ ist echt total abgedreht.
The guy is totally nuts.

schnallen
to understand; lit. to buckle, to strap
Der Kerl schnallt nicht, wie man eine Windel wechselt.
The guy doesn't have a clue of how to change a diaper.

hirnrissig
completely dumb, crazy; lit. crack-brained
Deine Idee ist komplett hirnrissig.
Your idea is completely dumb.

Dussel, m.
twit, dope
Manfred ist ein Dussel. Wir gehen zum Konzert und er vergisst unsere Tickets.
Manfred is a dope. We got to the concert and he forgot to bring our tickets.

Fatzke, m.
wise ass, stuck-up twit
Ich hasse es zu sagen, Sara, aber dein Freund ist ein arroganter Fatzke.
I hate to say it, Sara, but your boyfriend is an arrogant, stuck-up twit.

Klugscheißer, m.
smart-ass; lit. wisdom shitter

Du bist ein Klugscheißer!
You're a smart-ass!

Doktor Allwissend, m.
know-it-all; lit. Dr. Omniscient (based on the Brothers Grimm fable)
Mach hier nicht einen auf Doktor Allwissend.
Don't act like a know-it-all.

dumm wie Bohnenstroh sein
to be as dumb as a rock; lit. to be as dumb as a bundle of bean
straw
Er sieht gut aus, aber ist so dumm wie Bohnenstroh.
He's gorgeous, but as dumb as a rock.

zwei Dumme, ein Gedanke
literally; two fools, one thought (*when two people have the same
idea*)
**Klaus und Uwe sind beide Bier holen gegangen; da waren
zwei Dumme und ein Gedanke!**
Klaus and Uwe both went to get beer; two fools, one thought!

Nullchecker, m.
moron
**Dreimal habe ich versucht es dem Tim zu erklären, aber
er ist einfach ein Nullchecker, der es immer noch nicht
kapiert.**
*I tried to explain it to Tim three times, but he's such a moron he
still doesn't get it.*

raffen
to 'get' something; lit. to gather, to get
Paul hat gesagt, dass er die Matheaufgabe gar nicht rafft.
Paul said he doesn't get the math homework at all.

23

checken

to 'get' something

Ich liebe meine Mutter, aber sie checkt mich einfach nicht.

I love my mom, but she just doesn't get me.

There are many hip alternatives for the verb verstehen. *These include* peilen, kapieren, schnallen, blicken, checken, *and* raffen, *which are similar to "to get something/someone" and "to get someone's drift." If the term* nur Bahnhof verstehen, *lit. "to only understand train station," is Greek to you, then you're ahead of the game . . . that's exactly what it means!*

---

anscheißen

to scold/to yell

Ich hatte Streit mit meiner Freundin. Sie hat mich total angeschissen.

I had a fight with my girlfriend. She really gave me hell.

Bert, m.

idiot; actually an out-of-fashion first name

Du bist so ein Bert, dir muss man alles zweimal erklären.

You are such an idiot. You need everything to be explained twice.

astrein

to be one´s own man (for a person), to be cool (for a thing); lit. a clean branch

Der Film war astrein.

The movie was awesome.

Drecksack, m.

scumbag

Du bist ein echter Drecksack, wie du die Leute abgezockt hast.

What a scumbag you are, taking these people's money.

Drecksau, f.

filthy pig

Du Drecksau hast das schmutzige Geschirr von den letzten vier Tagen rumstehen.

You filthy pig, you've got four days' worth of dirty dishes lying around.

Dreckskerl, m.

dirty bastard

Der Dreckskerl hat mich einfach sitzen lassen.

That dirty bastard just walked out on me.

Donnerwetter!, n.

Darn it!; lit. thunder weather

Zum Donnerwetter! Jetzt sei endlich still!

Darn it! Just be quiet now!

rausreiten aus der Scheisse

to get out of deep shit

Sieh zu, wie du uns aus der Scheiße wieder rausreitest!

You got us into deep shit, now get us out of it!

CHAPTER FOUR

Du Schweinehund:

Words to Both Flatter and Insult

Sometimes, the beer is the warmest thing in Germany. If you arrive expecting friendly greetings and big smiles, you may be in for a disappointment. *Das Lächeln*, the smile, that centerpiece of American culture, is practically nonexistent in *Deutschland*. It may seem contradictory, but in fact Germans love to laugh and tend to have a well-developed sense of humor (unless of course, you're joking about their lack of smiling). In nearly every town, you'll find *Comedy-Clubs*, *Kabaretts*, and/or *Kleinkunstbühnen*, all of which are venues for many productions dedicated to joke-telling. Don't worry if you don't get the punchlines at first; after a *Stein* or two of 6 percent beer you'll be laughing your *Arsch* off.

But it gets worse. Many Germans consider Americans to be less than sincere or even superficial because they like to give compliments and kind remarks to people they don't necessarily know very well. So what we'd consider friendly, polite, and encouraging here is really too 'nice' for the Germans. On the other hand, Americans consider Germans impolite and discouraging because they don't compliment perfect strangers on their hairstyles or thank the cashier at Dunkin' Donuts profusely for throwing in an extra Munchkin.

Bär, m.

iron man, bodybuilder; lit. bear

Uwe ist voll der Bär; gegen den kannst du es nicht aufnehmen.

Uwe is an iron man; you don't stand a chance against him.

Hansdampf in allen Gassen, m.

Jack of all trades (and master of none); lit. Jack in all alleyways

Wie ein Hansampf in allen Gassen hat Johann allein in den letzten fünf Jahren als Feuerwehrmann, Frisör, Schreiner und Gebrauchtwagenhändler gearbeitet.

A real Jack of all trades, in just the past five years Johann has worked as a firefighter, hairdresser, carpenter, and used car salesman.

Zampano, m.

big shot

Volker spielt sich auf wie der große Zampano persönlich.

Volker always acts like a big shot.

The term Zampano comes from the 1954 film La Strada, or Das Lied der Strasse in German, by famed Italian director Federico Fellini. Der grosse Zampano (Italian Zampanò) is one of the three main figures of the film, in which a mentally challenged girl is sold by her parents to a traveling juggler named Zampano. He wants to make money off the girl and "breaks her in" for a show.

During the training he uses a whip and forces the girl to repeat over and over, "Ich bin der große Zampano," meaning "I am the great Zampano."

Today this term is used for a person who pulls all the strings.

toller Hecht, m.

talented guy, ace; lit. cool pike

Mark hat gestern wieder mal eine Eins bekommen—er ist ein toller Hecht.

Mark got another A yesterday—what an ace.

Hosenscheißer, m.

coward, chickenshit; lit. one who shits in his pants

Der Hossenscheisser hat sich verpisst.

The chickenshit got scared and left.

Schiss haben

to be afraid of someone or something

Ich habe so Schiss vor der morgigen Prüfung.

I'm so afraid of the test tomorrow.

Weichei, n.

wimp; lit. soft egg

Stell dich nich' so an, du Weichei!

Don't make such a fuss, you wimp!

Rindvieh, n.

moron; lit. bovine, cattle

In der Gegenmannschaft spielen lauter Rindviecher.

The opposite team is a bunch of morons.

Rotznase, f.
little snot, prick
Nicht mal danke hat diese Rotznase gesagt.
The little snot didn't even say thank you.

Scherzkeks, m.
joker, funny man; lit. funny cookie
Mich mit der Rechnung sitzen lassen. Haha, sehr witzig, du Scherzkeks.
Letting me get stuck with the bill. Haha, very funny, you joker!

beleidigte Leberwurst, f.
sulker; lit. the insulted liver sausage
Spiel mal nicht gleich die beleidigte Leberwurst!
You don't have to start sulking!
Lit. Don't play the insulted liver sausage!

der faule Sack, m.
lazy bum
Du fauler Sack könntest auch mal den Abfall rausbringen.
You could take the garbage out once in a while, you lazy bum.

jemandem auf den Sack gehen
to get on someone's nerves
Deine kleine Schwester geht mir total auf den Sack.
Your little sister gets on my nerves.

Poser, m.
showoff
Das ist nur ein Poser, nix dahinter!
He's just a showoff, all talk no action!

rolexen

to brag; lit. "to rolex" (from the famously expensive brand of watches)

Hör mit dem rolexen auf. Ist doch peinlich.

Stop bragging—it's embarrassing.

Fuzzi, m.

nerd

Ich finde die Bank-Fuzzis und Versicherungsfuzzis in ihren Anzügen zum Totlachen.

I could laugh myself silly at these nerdy bank and insurance guys in their suits.

schnorren

to mooch; lit. to sponge off someone

Darf ich 'ne Kippe von dir schnorren?

Can I mooch a cigarette from you?

Schnorrbert, m.

mooch; actually a combination of the old-fashioned name "Norbert" and the verb "schnorren"

Klaus ist ein Schnorrbert: will immer was haben, aber selber nix geben.

Klaus is a mooch: always wanting something, never giving back.

Freibiergesicht, n.

freeloader; lit. free-beer face

Die Hälfte der Gäste habe ich gar nicht eingeladen, aber auf Parties da sammeln sich die Freibiergesichter.

I didn't invite half of these people, but a lot of freeloaders show up at parties.

ablästern

to talk shit

Amber lästerte über ihn ab, nachdem sie sich getrennt hatten.

Amber talked shit about her fiancé after they broke up.

Macho, m.

macho man

Jens ist ein alter Macho, der schickt seine Freudin zum Bier holen.

Jens is an old macho man. He sends his girlfriend to get beer.

Arsch mit Ohren, m.

idiot; lit. ass with ears

Hast Du gesehen, wie der mich von rechts überholt hat? Der fährt wie ein echter Arsch mit Ohren.

Did you see how that guy passed me on the right? This guy drives like an idiot.

Torte, f.

tart

Du glaubt doch nicht, dass du 'ne Chance bei der Torte hast?

You don't really think you have a chance with this tart, do you?

Sahne, f.

bomb, first class; lit. cream

Die Party gestern war erste Sahne!

Last night's party was the bomb!

Sahneschnitte, f.

peach; lit. cream puff

Boah, schau mal die zwei Sahneschnitten dort drüben. Lass uns mal hallo sagen.

Wow, do you see the two peaches over there? Let's go say hi.

Sau, f.
bitch, bastard
Ich rede nicht mehr mit der Sau!
I don't talk to that bitch anymore.

Sau- prefix
damn, lousy
Die Sauarbeit im Garten in diesem Sauwetter geht mir auf's Gemüt.
This damn gardening work in this lousy weather is getting on my nerves.

Schwein, n.
pig, bastard, son of a bitch
Das Schwein hat den ganzen Abend mit 'ner Anderen rumgemacht, während seine Freundin mit Grippe im Bett lag.
The pig flirted all night with another woman while his girlfriend was in bed with the flu.

Schwein haben
to be lucky; lit. to have swine
Wir haben Schwein gehabt.
We got lucky.

Schweinerei, f.
mess, scandal, dirty trick, indecent act; lit. pigsty
So eine Schweinerei!
How disgusting!
What a dirty trick!

Schmacko, m.
dream boat
Ich hab 'nen neuen Kollegen, n' richtiger Schmacko.
I have a new co-worker, a real dream boat.

Schnitzel, n.

hottie; lit. the cutlet

Im Urlaub hab ich ein richtiges Schnitzel kennengelernt. Leider wohnt er in Italien.

I met a real hottie on vacation. Unfortunately, he lives in Italy.

abartig

drop-dead; lit. deviant or unnatural

Verdammt, du bist so abartig schön!

Damn, you are drop-dead beautiful!

hammerhart

groovy, amazing; lit. hard as a hammer

Du siehst so hammerhart aus, dass mir echt die Worte fehlen!

You look so amazing that I'm speechless!

CHAPTER FIVE

In der Eile:

A Question of Time

In the United States, it's "In God We Trust," but the Germans take this one step further, putting their faith in every citizen. Public transportation in Germany, Switzerland, and Austria works on the honor system, and everyone, from mangy punk rockers to the president, buys a ticket. Don't think you can outsmart the system, as undercover agents patrol the subway, streetcars, and buses and can demand that you produce your ticket at any time. If you do decide to take a chance with *Schwarzfahren*, literally "riding black," carry an extra wad of bills with you—fines vary, but you can count on paying the equivalent of fifteen beers or a blow job (at current exchange rates, 60 euros).

Going by foot? You'll still need to bring your *Brieftasche* along. Setting a proper example for youngsters is paramount in Germany. No matter if it's midnight on a Saturday and most kiddies are fast asleep in their beds. Crossing the street on a red light in Germany elicits approximately the same reaction as, say, vehicular manslaughter in the United States. If you are lucky, you'll be scolded by an old *Grossi*, granny, out walking her ugly little poodle. If you are caught by the police, though, you'll be fined up to 25 euros on the spot.

Ab geht die Post!

Off you (we) go!; lit. The post is leaving!

Noch zwei Wochen bis zum Urlaub und dann ab geht die Post nach Puerto Rico.

Two more weeks until vacation, and then off we go to Puerto Rico.

los

go

Achtung, fertig, los!

On your mark, get set, go!

halblang

easy, not so fast; lit. half long

Jetzt mach mal halblang!

Take it easy!

aus dem Quark kommen

to get a slow start; lit. to come out of the cheese

Es ist schon fast Mittag. Kommst du jetzt endlich aus dem Quark und stehst auf?

It's almost noon already. Are you finally going to get up and going, or what?

den Arsch hochkriegen

to get one's ass in gear

Krieg endlich deinen Arsch hoch, sonst ist die Kacke am Dampfen!

Get your ass in gear or the shit will really hit the fan!

lahmarschig

slow-poke; lit. slow-assed

**Der Alex ist so lahmarschig. Auf den muss man stunden-
lang warten.**
*Alex is such a slow-poke. You always have to wait for him for
hours.*

Kurve kratzen, f.
to hit the road; lit. to scratch the bend
**Was, schon so spät? Jetzt muss ich aber schnell die Kurve
kratzen.**
What, is it already so late? I gotta hit the road now.

Affenzahn, m.
mad speed; lit. monkey tooth
Ich bin im Affenzahn dahin gerast.
I drove at a mad speed.

dalli, dalli
chop, chop; hurry up
Dalli, dalli oder wir verpassen den Anfang des Films.
Hurry up or we'll miss the beginning of the movie.

Mach zu!
hurry, get on with it; lit. close it
Mach zu! Der Bus fährt gleich ab.
Hurry! The bus is about to leave.

*Speaking of getting going, here are a few examples of
phrases that make perfect sense in German, but seem a
little screwy to English speakers:*

Wir müssen uns langsam beeilen.
We have to get going; lit. we have to slowly hurry.
(Exactly how do you hurry slowly?)
Warte mal schnell.
Just wait a second; lit. wait quickly.
Das ist ja schön blöd.
That is incredibly stupid; lit. this is beautifully stupid.
Geh, bleib da! Austria and Bavaria.
Please stay; lit. Go, don't leave!
Du solltest lieber ganz schnell langsam fahren.
You'd better slow down immediately; lit. you should very fast go slow.

wie eine gesengte Sau fahren
to drive like a fucking maniac; lit. to drive like a singed sow
Sie fahren wie'ne gesengte Sau!
You drive like a fucking maniac!

heizen
to speed; lit. to heat
Auf der Strecke kann man so richtig schön heizen.
On this road you can really go fast.

brettern
to hurtle, to race; lit. to board up something
Ein Standard Mercedes kann mit 130 Meilen pro Stunde über die Autobahn brettern.
A standard Mercedes can race down the highway at 130 miles an hour.

kacheln

to speed; lit. to tile

Ich muss morgen nach München. Da werde ich schön die A9 runterkacheln.

I have to go to Munich tomorrow. I'll race down the A9 [Highway 9].

Die Autobahn, *Germany's network of highways, is often mistakenly thought to be the world's oldest. That honor actually goes to Italy, as their Milan-Varese autoway opened in 1929, three years before the first section of the Autobahn. Sadly, that seems to be the last year Italy did any maintenance on the road as well. Germany is the only European country that has no speed limit on its highways (at least on some stretches)—and recent attempts to install one have been voted down by the public. Germans have a great love for their cars and are especially proud to be the homeland of Mercedes, BMW, and Volkswagen. Wherever you go, you are never more than a stone's throw from a car factory, museum, car wash, or dealership.*

heißer Ofen, m.

motorcycle, hot rod; lit. hot oven

Ich würde gern mal deinen heissen Ofen auf 'ne Probefahrt nehmen.

I'd love to take your hot rod for a spin.

Blechlawine, f.

long line of backed-up cars, traffic jam; lit. metal avalanche

Wir haben heute auf der Autobahn eine riesige Blechlawine gesehen.

On the highway today we saw a huge traffic jam.

Autoschlange, f.

traffic jam; lit. car snake

Tut mir leid, dass ich zu spät komme, aber ich hab fast zwei Stunden in einer Autoschlange gesessen.

Sorry I'm late, but I was caught in traffic for nearly two hours.

Lappen, m.

driver's license; llit. rag, cloth (German driver's licenses were once made of large gray paper folded in half.)

Dem Fritz haben sie seinen Lappen weggenommen.

They took away Fritz's driver's license.

Knolle, f. or Knöllchen, n.

ticket; from *Protokoll*, lit. protocol

Mein Bruder hat gestern seine zehnte Knolle bekommen.

My brother got his tenth speeding ticket yesterday.

Knolle *is colloquial for* Strafmandat, *"ticket," and is a malapropism of the word* Protokoll.

Knöllchen *is the diminutive of* Knolle. *A possible explanation for the term is that when you get one, you're so annoyed you crumple it up (*zusammenknüllen*) and throw it on the backseat.*

Drahtesel, m.
bike; lit. a wire donkey
Mein Drahtesel bringt mich überall hin und spart Energie.
My bike takes me everywhere and saves energy.

Dingsbums, n.
thingy, whatchamacallit
Dagmar, kannst du mir mal das Dingsbums reichen?
Dagmar, can you hand me the whatchamacallit?

CHAPTER SIX

Es schmeckt nach mehr:

Food, Glorious Food

Dinner in a German-speaking household can be a new experience for Americans, whose table manners pale in comparison. Number one, be sure to keep both your hands out of your lap and on the table at all times. Perverts that they are, the Germans, Swiss, and Austrians won't believe you if you claim you're just resting your hand on your napkin. So unless you want to choke the chicken rather than eat the one being served, remember this important rule.

Number two, Germans, like most Europeans, eat "backwards," with the knife held in the right hand and the fork in the left. Even sillier, the fork is often put into the mouth upside-down after stabbing a bite of food this way. Your dinner companions will even use their knife to shove more food onto the upside-down fork. Should you try to fit in by emulating your hosts, beware—you may want to practice at home first to ensure you don't break a tooth.

Essen fassen
to grab a bite
Komm Sven, lass uns Essen fassen.
Come on Sven, let's grab a bite.

einen Kohldampf haben

to be ravenous; lit. to have a cabbage vapor
Mann, hab ich einen Kohldampf.
Boy, am I ravenous.

> Don't get grossed out if a German tells you "Ich habe
> Kohldampf." His "cabbage vapor" has nothing to do with
> the fine smells that can invade a room after several help-
> ings of Sauerkraut. Kohldampf *comes from two eighteenth-
> century thieves' terms for hunger,* Kohl *and* Dampf.

ein Loch im Bauch haben

to be starving; lit. to have a hole in the belly
Mittagspause! Mann, hab ich ein Loch im Bauch.
Lunch break! Man, am I starving.

fressen

to eat, to pig out; lit. to gorge
**Georg frisst Unmengen Hamburger und Pommes, aber das
Gemüse rührt er nicht an.**
*Georg gorges on hamburgers and fries, but he won't touch the
vegetables.*

futtern

to stuff one's face
Hör auf zu futtern und lass noch was für die anderen übrig.
Stop stuffing your face and leave something for the rest of us.

futtern wie ein Scheunendrescher

to eat like a horse; lit. to eat like a threshing machine

Jon frisst wie ein Scheunendrescher.
Jon eats like a horse.

wegspachteln
to polish off
Der Martin kann einen ganzen Käsekuchen allein wegspachteln.
Martin can polish off an entire cheesecake by himself.

naschen
to snack, to nosh
Ich habe so viel genascht, dass ich keinen Hunger aufs Abendessen habe.
I snacked so much that I'm not hungry for dinner.

mit jemandem ein Hühnchen zu rupfen haben
to have a bone to pick with someone; lit. to have a young chicken to pluck with someone
Ich muss ein Hühnchen rupfen mit dem Kerl, der mir mein Fahrrad geklaut hat.
I've got a bone to pick with the guy who stole my new bike.

jemandem die Suppe versalzen
to spoil things for someone; lit. to oversalt someone's soup
Konstanze freute sich auf die Party, aber ihre Mutter hat ihr mit Hausarrest die Suppe versalzen.
Konstanze was looking forward to the party, but her mother grounded her and spoiled her plans.

eine Naschkatze sein
to have a sweet tooth; lit. to be a snack cat

Henriette mag Schokolade, Gummibärchen, Kekse—eine richtige Naschkatze eben.
Henriette likes chcocolate, gummy bears, cookies—she has a real sweet tooth.

Heißhunger auf etwas haben
to have a craving for something; lit. to have hot-hunger for something
Ich habe jetzt einen Heißhunger auf Pizza.
I've got a craving for pizza right now.

reinhauen
to dig in
Als die Pizza endlich ankam, haben wir richtig reingehauen.
When the pizza finally came, we dug right in.

das Faustbrötchen
knuckle sandwich; lit. fist sandwich
Lorentz und Fred mussten während der Schlägerei mehrere Faustbrötchen essen.
Lorentz and Fred had to eat a few knuckle sandwiches during the fight.

kein Kostverächter sein
bon vivant, French for someone who lives well and likes to have a good time; lit. one who doesn't turn down good food
Was Frauen anbelangt ist Günther kein Kostverächter.
Günther is a bon vivant when it comes to women.

sich vollgefressen fühlen
to be stuffed

Ich kriege keinen Bissen mehr runter. Ich fühl mich so vollgefressen.
I can't take one more bite. I'm stuffed.

jemandem das Wasser im Mund zusammenlaufen
to make someone's mouth water
Beim Anblick der Schweinshaxe lief Wilhelm das Wasser im Mund zusammen.
The sight of the pork knuckle made Wilhelm's mouth water.

dinieren
to be wined and dined
Im Urlaub haben wir wunderschön diniert.
On vacation we were wined and dined.

ein gefundenes Fressen sein
to be an easy target; lit. to be a found feast
Ihr Misserfolg war ein gefundenes Fressen für ihre politischen Gegner.
Her mishap was an easy target for her political opponents.

aus der Hand fressen
to be wrapped around someone's little finger; lit. eating out of the palm of the hand
Er frisst ihr aus der Hand.
She's got him wrapped around her little finger.

den Braten riechen
to know what's up; lit. to smell the roast
Trotz aller Versuche seiner Frau ihre Affäre zu verheimlichen hat Jason den Braten gerochen.
Despite his wife's attempt to hide her affair, Jason knew what was up.

This phrase goes back to the fable of the farmer who invited a pig for dinner. The pig arrived at the door, got a whiff of the aromas coming from the kitchen, and realized that a fellow pig was cooking as pork roast. Not surprisingly, the pig preferred to leave on an empty stomach.

sich den Bauch vollschlagen
to stuff oneself; lit. to hit the belly until it's full
Wir haben uns den Bauch mit Eiscreme und Torte vollgeschlagen.
We stuffed ourselves with ice cream and cake.

verschlingen
to devour
Ich könnte ein halbes Schwein verschlingen.
I could devour half a pig.

In the state of Lower Saxony, Schwein *levels have hit the eight million mark . . . and no, that doesn't include the local population. The Germans currently rank number four in worldwide per capita pork consumption and most* Leute *could wolf down a* Wurst *anytime, night or day.*

Mahlzeit, f.
Bon appétit, have a nice meal; lit. mealtime
Der Spruch "Mahlzeit" wird ausgesprochen, wenn jemanden zu spät ins Büro kommt, oder einfach wenn man sich "Guten Appetit" wünschen möchte.

"Mahlzeit" is said either to someone who walks into the office late for work, or is used to say "Have a good meal" at the beginning of any meal apart from breakfast.

Kalorien tanken, pl.

to eat fast food; lit. to tank up on calories

Hey, ich könnte jetzt ein paar Kalorien tanken gehen.

Hey, I could go for some fast food right now.

Mafiatörtchen, n.

pizza; lit. mafia tart

Im Ciao Bella gibt's die besten Mafiatörtchen.

Ciao Bella has the best pizza.

A-Saft or O-Saft, m.

apple juice or orange juice

Möchtest Du A-Saft oder O-Saft?

Would you like some apple juice or orange juice?

lecker

yummy, delicious

Das war lecker.

That was yummy.

ekelhaft

disgusting, scuzzy

Dass du am Esstisch gerülpst hast war ekelhaft.

It was disgusting that you burped at the dinner table.

Döner, m.

doner kebab

Der Döner hat die Bratwurst als Imbiss abgelöst.

The doner kebab has replaced the bratwurst as a snack.

CHAPTER SEVEN

Zuerst kommt ein Bier und dann noch ein Bier:

Germany's Liquid Gold

Germany is one of the cheapest places in Europe to buy beer, but also the most difficult in which to make a choice—there are over 1,500 different brands and types of beer! Germans do really love beer; they rank second worldwide in beer consumption per person, after Ireland. In Bavaria, for example, beer is officially considered a food. Accordingly, "brewsky slang" has developed over the years, putting beer center stage in several popular expressions. If you attempt to join in a conversation but someone says *Das ist nicht dein Bier*, be sure to mind your own business. If the situation continues to deteriorate, you might soon hear *Bei ihm ist Hopfen und Malz verloren*, lit. "hops and malt are lost on him," meaning you're a lost cause, beyond all hope.

What does a German drink after drinking a lot of beer? That's right: more beer! The most common request in any *Gasthaus* or beer hall is *noch eins*—another one.

Kneipe, f.
corner bar, local bar
Ich bin Stammgast in meiner Eckkneipe.
I'm a regular at my local bar.

Pulle, f.
bottle
Reich mal die Pulle rüber.
Hand over the bottle.

abschädeln
to booze it up
Walter: "Wie bitte, das Bier kost nur 'n Euro und der Korn 80 cent, da können wir uns von unseren 30 Euros ja richtig gut abschädeln!"
Walter: "What? The beer here is one euro and the schnapps 80 cents. With our 30 euros we can really booze it up here!"

ein Bier zischen
to have a beer; lit. to hiss (maybe from the sound a can of beer makes when opened)
Stefan geht mit seinen Freunden noch ein Bier zischen.
Stefan is going to have one more beer with his friends.

abschießen
to be hammered; lit. to fire off, to down
Boah, der Rolf hat sich aber gestern abgeschossen; der konnte nicht mehr gerade stehen.
Man, Rolf was hammered last night; he couldn't stand up straight anymore.

Herrenhandtäschchen, n.
six pack; lit. a man's handbag
Hey Jungs, habt ihre eure Herrenhandtäschchen dabei?
Guys, did you bring your six packs?

Schluckwunder, n.
drunk; lit. the swallowing wonder

Mann, du hattest gestern acht Bier—bist'n richtiges Schluckwunder.

Dude, you had eight beers yesterday—you're a drunk.

Blechbrötchen, n.

can of beer; lit. tin sandwich

Schmeiß ma ein Blechbrötchen rüber.

Yo, toss me a can of beer.

Brauereitumor, m.

beer belly; lit. brewery tumor

Wenn ich nicht bald mehr Sport mache, kriege ich einen Brauereitumor.

If I don't start working out more soon, I'm gonna get a beer belly.

Bölkstoff, m.

booze

Haben wir genügend Bölkstoff?

Do we have enough booze?

Château Migraine, m.

cheap wine; lit. migraine castle

Servier mir keinen Château Migraine, sonst drink ich lieber Wasser.

Don't give me any cheap wine, I'd rather drink water.

Pennerglück, n.

cheap alcohol

Was für'n Depp.

Peter kann sich nur Pennerglück leisten.

Peter can only afford cheap alcohol.

einen Brand haben

to be very thirsty; lit. to have a fire

Mann, hab ich einen Brand, ich könnte drei Liter Wasser wegtrinken.

I'm so thirsty I could drink three liters of water.

Alk, m.

alcohol, abbreviation for alcohol

Ich sollte echt keinen Alk mehr trinken.

I should give up alcohol.

zu tief ins Glas gucken

to have one too many; lit. to look too deeply into the glass

Manchmal guckt Andrea zu tief ins Glas.

Occasionally, Andrea has one too many.

zu sein

to be sloshed; lit. to be closed

Drei Bier und er ist schon zu!

Three beers and he's already sloshed!

There are plenty more terms for being smashed and hammered, for example the following, with their literal meanings:

lattenstramm—*sturdy as a crossbar*
rabenvoll—*full as a raven*
rattendicht—*dense like a rat*
breit sein—*to be wide*
einen im Tee haben—*to have one in the tea*
einen in der Krone haben—*to have one in the crown*

> *The expression* Kurvenschuhe anhaben—*to wear crooked shoes—reveals one side effect of being smashed.*

Säufer, m.; Säuferin, f.
heavy drinker, alcoholic
Mein Vater ist ein Säufer.
My father is a heavy drinker.

Schluckspecht, m.
boozer; lit. swallowing woodpecker
Deine Freunde sind doch alle Schluckspechte.
All your friends are boozers.

Alkoholfahne, f.
to reek of alcohol; lit. alcohol flag
John hatte eine Alkoholfahne während des Vorstellungsgesprächs.
John reeked of alcohol during his interview.

Kampftrinken, n.
binge drinking; lit. battle drinking
Das Kampftrinken vieler Jugendlicher ist derzeit in der deutschen Presse.
Binge drinking among youth is the latest worry in the German press.

Alkoholleiche, f.
someone who is passed out; lit. alcohol corpse
Wer ist denn die Alkoholleiche auf der Couch?
Who is that passed out on the couch?

Trinksprüeche—Toasts:
Auf Ex! or Ex und hopp!—*Bottoms up!*
Erst mach' dein' Sach dann trink' und lach!—*First take care of business, then drink and laugh!*
Arbeit ist der Fluch der trinkenden Klasse.—*Work is the curse of the drinking class.*

sich die Kante geben
to get shit-faced; lit. to give oneself the edge
Heute werd ich mir mal ordentlich die Kante geben!
I'm going to get shit-faced tonight!

jemanden abfüllen
to get someone drunk; lit. to fill someone up
Auf der Party hat Klara ihren Freund richtig abgefüllt.
Klara got her boyfriend drunk at the party.
Lit. Klara filled up her boyfriend at the party.

saufen
to drink to excess, to booze
Christa ist sauer auf Robert, weil er jeden Freitagabend mit seinen Freunden saufen geht.
Christa is mad at Robert because he goes out drinking with his friends every Friday night.

Saufkumpane, pl.
drinking buddies
Bring bloß nicht deine Saufkumpane heim.
Don't you dare bring your drinking buddies home with you.

53

Zechbruder, m.
drinking buddy
Paul ist mein liebster Zechbruder.
Paul is my favorite drinking buddy.

Suff, m.
drunk
Im Suff sind alle Frauen schön!
When you're drunk, all women are beautiful!

Getting drunk in Germany is not frowned upon, but do not attempt to drive if you've had too much. There is no tolerance for drinking and driving, the alcohol limits are low, and the penalties are severe. Here are some particularly colorful expressions for drinking:

auf die Lampe gießen—*to water the lamp*
die Gurgel ölen—*to oil the throat*
einen schmettern—*to belt one out, to blare*
einen zur Brust nehmen—*to take one to the chest*
einen heben—*to lift one (a glass, a beer)*
einen hinter die Binde kippen—*to pour a drink behind the collar.*

Brot stemmen
to have a beer; lit. to lift bread
Komm, wir stemmen noch'n Brot!
Come on, let's have another beer!

Other Spirits

Puffbrause, f.
bubbly; lit. brothel lemonade
Ich drink lieber Bier. Von Puffbrause krieg' ich Kopfschmerz.
I prefer beer. Bubbly gives me a headache.

Absacker, m.
night cap; lit. sagger
Noch einen Absacker bevor wir heimgehen.
Let's have one more night cap before heading home.

Herrengedeck, n.
one glass of beer and one glass of sparkling wine or schnapps; lit. a gentleman's place setting (often sold in nightclubs to keep the beer-only crowd at bay by forcing them to buy more expensive drinks)
"Was darf's denn sein? " "Ein Herrengedeck bitte! "
"What can I get you?" "A beer and a shot."

Kurze, m.
schnapps; lit. short one
Noch eine Runde Kurze zum Auffrischen.
We need another round of schnapps to freshen up.

Magenbitter, m.
digestive; lit. stomach bitters
Nach diesem fettigen Essen brauche ich jetzt einen Magenbitter.
After that greasy food I need a digestive.

auf ex
bottoms up
Auf ex Freunde, der Letzte gibt ne' Runde aus!
Bottoms up, guys. The loser pays the next round!

göbeln
to vomit
Wer hat die Toilette vollgegöbelt?
Who threw up all over the toilet?

strullen
to piss
Boah, nach den fünf Bier muss ich erst mal strullen wie ein Polizeipferd!
Wow, after five beers I gotta piss like a racehorse.

Klo, n.
john
Das Klo ist schon seit zehn Minuten besetzt.
Someone's been on the john for ten minutes.

Topf, m.
can, lit. pot
Ich muss dringend auf den Topf.
I gotta use the can.

einen Kater haben
hangover; lit. to have a tom cat
Mann, habe ich 'nen Kater.
Man, I have such a hangover.

CHAPTER EIGHT

Wie geht's?:

Expressing Your Ups and Downs

When Germans ask *Wie geht es Ihnen?*—"How are you?—it is not just a polite greeting. The actual meaning of this phrase contrasts with the Stateside custom of asking "How's it going?" or "How are you?" when saying "Hi." If you ask a German *Wie geht's?* you will be told in great detail how they are doing. This might include any number of aches, pains, and descriptions of bodily functions. Some people might tell you the reasons why they are not feeling well, i.e. "My cat has a heart murmur and now the vet has to come up with treatment options and I'm so worried and upset." So for the most part, just say "*Hallo*" and keep on moving.

But as language is alive and constantly involving, the Americanization of *Wie geht's?* as a casual greeting is slowly catching on, something many Germans find superficial. That isn't your fault (even though they may look at you like it is). If Germans practiced their old hobbies of *cuckoo* clock making and sausage grinding instead of watching reruns of Jerry Springer and listening to Britney, they could probably retain more of their polite, cultured ways.

sich fühlen als ob man Bäume ausreißen könnte
to be ready to take on/do anything; lit. to feel as if one could rip out trees
Die Konferenz lief wie am Schnürchen und jetzt geht's mir als könnte ich Bäume ausreißen.
The meeting went like clockwork and now I'm ready to take on anything.

unbekümmert
happy-go-lucky
Wie kannst du nur so unbekümmert sein, wenn dein Job in Gefahr ist?
How can you be so happy-go-lucky if your job is on the line?

Bombenstimmung, f.
terrific mood, high spirits; lit. bombing mood
Auf der Weihnachtsfeier waren alle in Bombenstimmung.
At the Christmas party, everyone was in a terrific mood.

super drauf sein
to do/be very well, be in top form
Die Fußballmannschaft war super drauf und gewann fünf zu null.
The soccer team did very well and won five to zero.

im grünen Bereich sein
to have everything under control; lit. to be in the green sector (the opposite of a red alert)
Keine Angst, hier ist alles im grünen Bereich.
Don't worry, everything is under control.

Wolke sieben
cloud nine; lit. cloud seven

Nachdem Bryan und Claudia sich geküsst hatten, waren sie auf Wolke sieben.
After Bryan and Claudia kissed, they were on cloud nine.

fit wie ein Turnschuh sein
to be as fit as a fiddle; lit. to be as fit as a sneaker
Mein Opa war lange krank, aber mittlerweile ist er schon wieder fit wie ein Turnschuh.
My grandpa was sick for a long time, but now he's fit as a fiddle again.

blendend gehen
to be doing great, fantastic
Nach meiner Scheidung geht's mir blendend.
Since my divorce, I'm doing great.

aus dem Häuschen sein
to be out of one's mind, ecstatic; lit. to be out of the house
Nach dem Lottogewinn war Mutti total aus dem Häuschen.
After she won the lottery, mom was out of her mind.

leben wie eine Made im Speck
to live in the lap of luxury; lit. to live like a maggot in bacon
Du kannst auch nicht immer wie die Made im Speck leben.
You can't always live in the lap of luxury.

Wutanfall, m.
temper tantrum
Gerhardts häufige Wutanfälle zerstörten seine Beziehung.
Gerhardt's frequent temper tantrums destroyed his relationship.

hitzig werden
to lose one's temper; lit. to get heated

In Auseinandersetzungen kann sie sehr hitzig werden.
She's prone to lose her temper in discussions.

vor Wut kochend
in a rage; lit. cooking with rage
Vor Wut kochend verließ er das Zimmer.
He left the room in a rage.

platt sein or platt machen
to be flabbergasted; lit. to be (or make someone) flat
Deine Neuigkeiten machen mich platt.
I'm flabbergasted by your news.

sich daneben fühlen
to feel off; lit. to stand beside oneself
Seit ein paar Tagen schon fühle ich mich daneben.
For days now, I've being feeling off.

angepisst
pissed
Karsten ist total angepisst, dass Regina mit 'nem anderen Kerl flirtet.
Karsten is really pissed off that Regina is flirting with another guy.

Arschlochkarte ziehen
to get the short end of the stick; lit. to pull the asshole card
Frank wurde aufgefordert den Bilanzbericht zu schreiben. Damit hat er echt die Arschlochkarte gezogen.
Frank was asked to put together the status report. He really got the short end of the stick.

Hass kriegen
to get extremely annoyed; lit. to get hatred

Noch mehr Überstunden ohne Bezahlung? Da kannst du echt den Hass kriegen.

More overtime without pay? This is getting extremely annoying.

Another expression for this state of mind is Ich hab so'n Hals, *meaning I'm really angry, lit. I have such a neck. When saying this, be sure to show the huge swollen lymph nodes in your neck by putting your hands on either side.*

---

durchknallen

to lose it; lit. to blow through
Dem Thorsten ist eine Birne durchgeknallt.
Thorsten just lost it.
Lit. One of Thorsten's bulbs blew.

rumhängen or abhängen

to hang out
Ach, ich hänge heute schon die ganze Zeit nur so rum.
Well, I pretty much hung out all day today.

jucken

to care; lit. to itch
Mich juckt es gar nicht, wenn ich dich nicht mehr sehe!
I don't care at all if I don't see you again!
Lit. It doesn't itch me at all if I don't see you again!

abschimmeln

to be bored; lit. to molder away
Wir sind gestern nur abgeschimmelt und haben nichts Produktives gemacht.
We were bored yesterday and didn't do anything productive.

61

cremig bleiben

to remain cool; lit. to stay creamy

Mario blieb trotz der Prüfung ganz cremig und machte sich keinen Stress.

Despite the exam, Mario stayed cool and didn't stress out.

Schadenfreude, f.

happiness at the misfortune of others

Er empfand Schadenfreude, als er hörte, dass seine Ex, die kürzlich mit ihm Schluss gemacht hatte, nun selbst von ihrem Neuen sitzen gelassen wurde.

He was pleased when he heard that the girl who recently dumped him had just been dumped by her new boyfriend.

abfahren auf etwas

to find something awesome; lit. to take off on something

Ich bin voll auf die neue CD von Black 47 abgefahren.

I think the new Black 47 CD is awesome.

fertig sein

to be beat or exhausted; lit. to be finished

Hab heute den ganzen Tag an meinem Referat gearbeitet und bin nun total fertig.

I worked the entire day on my presentation and now I'm completely beat.

umhauen

to blow someone's mind; lit. to knock out

Das Konzert hat mich umgehauen.

The concert blew my mind.

CHAPTER NINE

Intelligenz plus Faulheit gleich Effizienz:

Yes, You Do Need an Education

Education, including college, is practically free in Germany. While some students manage to finish their degrees in the required maximum time of six years, many more enjoy years of of beer swilling and partying with just an occasional class on the side. Partially as a result of this, some German universities initiated fees of up to a thousand euros per year in 2005. More recently, in 2006/2007, several states started charging everyone what we would call tuition, from their first semester on, of about 1,000 euros per year. Sounds like chump change to us, but some 10,000 students in five cities protested the new fees—and sadly, their budgets had to account for several hundred fewer beers.

Upon graduation, students used to find well-paid jobs as giant pretzel bakers or tuba players immediately. For the past decade though, *Deutschland* has suffered from a high unemployment rate, around ten percent. While some say this is the fault of lazy students or an abundance of foreigners, it is more likely a sign of the times.

schwänzen
to play hooky, to ditch
Peter und Natalie wurden beim Schule schwänzen erwischt.
Peter and Natalie got caught playing hooky.

sich von Dr. Holiday krankschreiben lassen
to play hooky; lit. to get a sick note from Dr. Holiday
Lars fehlt heute schon wieder. Der hat sich vom Dr. Holiday krankschreiben lassen!
Lars is out again today. He's playing hooky!
Lit. Lars is out again today. He got a sick note from Dr. Holiday!

blau machen
to skip work or school; lit. to make blue
Ich mache heute blau.
I'm skipping work today.

Penne, f.
school
Ich hab die Penne so satt.
I'm so tired of school.

Spickzettel, pl.
cheat sheets; lit. crib notes
Mit seinen Spickzetteln mogelt sich Thomas durch alle Klausuren.
With his cheat sheets, Thomas cheats his way through every test.

Schummler, m.
cheater
Ich spiele nicht mehr mit Uwe. Der ist ein alter Schummler.
I don't want to play with Uwe anymore. He's a cheater.

mogeln
to cheat, to fudge
Ich habe bei den Antworten gemogelt.
I fudged my answers a little bit.

abkupfern
to crib, to copy
Annette hat die Hausaufgabe von mir abgekupfert.
Annette copied the entire homework from me.

schleimen
to suck up; lit. to slime
Die Susanne schleimt sich bei allen Lehrer ein.
Susanne sucks up to all the teachers.

Prof, m. or f.
university professor
Mein Geschichtsprof hat mindestens zehn Bücher geschrieben.
My history professor has written at least ten books.

Hiwi, m. or f. (abbr. of Hilfswissenschaftler)
university assistant
Die Hiwis müssen die ganze Kurserecherche machen.
It's the university assistants who have to do all the course research.

nicht die leiseste Ahnung von etwas haben
to not have about the slightest clue about something
Und du dachtest, wir hätten nicht die leiseste Ahnung!
And you thought we didn't have the slightest clue!

in den sauren Apfel beißen
to bite the bullet; lit. to bite into the sour apple

Wir müssen wohl in den sauren Apfel beißen und die Mieterhöhung zahlen, schließlich können wir nicht einfach umziehen.
We'll have to bite the bullet and pay the increased rent; after all, we just can't move.

Grips im Kopf haben
to have plenty up top
Niemand glaubt's, aber Heiner hat 'ne Menge Grips im Kopf.
Nobody believes it, but Heiner has plenty up top.

pauken
to cram
Habe heute keine Zeit zum Einkaufen. Ich muss für den Englischtest pauken.
I don't have time for shopping today. I have to cram for the English test.

Schlaumeier, m.
wise guy
Herman hat in der Schule immer Ärger gekriegt, weil er so ein Schlaumeier war.
Herman got always into trouble in school because he was such a wise guy.

so tun, als hätte man die Weisheit mit dem Löffel gegessen
to act as if one knows all the answers; lit. to act as if one had eaten wisdom with a spoon
Dein neuer Macker tut auch so, als hätte er die Weisheit mit dem Löffel gegessen und wenn du ihn dann was fragst, hat er Mattscheibe.
Your new beau thinks he has all the answers, but when you ask him something, he blanks.

durchfallen
to fail; lit. to fall through
Uschi ist durch die Fahrprüfung gefallen.
Uschi failed her driver's test.

etwas schmeißen
to drop out of something, to ditch; lit. to throw something
Ich habe meine Philosophievorlesung geschmissen. Die war einfach zu langweilig.
I dropped out of my philosophy class. It was just too boring.

einen Abschluss machen
to graduate; lit. to make a degree or conclusion
Ich hoffe bald meinen Abschluss zu machen.
I hope to graduate soon.

gut in etwas abschneiden
to do well; lit. to cut off well
Die Schwimmerin hat bei ihrem Wettkampf sehr gut abgeschnitten.
The swimmer did very well in her race.

abhartzen
to work very hard
Tut mir leid, dass du selbst am Wochenende so abhartzen must. Mach doch mal Pause.
I'm sorry you have to work so hard, even on weekends. You should take a break.

jemanden knechten
to break someone's chops, to reem someone's ass; lit. to subjugate or rule over

Mein Chef hat mich heute wieder übelst knechten lassen.
My boss broke my chops in the worst way again today.

Other slang terms for arbeiten *(to work) are:* schuften, abaxten *(lit. to axe), and* malochen. Malochen *is a Yiddish term for work.*

ein großes Tier sein

to be a big shot; lit. to be a big animal
Mein Onkel ist ein ganz großes Tier in der Bankbranche.
My uncle is a big shot in the banking industry.

jemandem auf den Schlips treten

to step on one's toes; lit. to step on someone's tie
Ernsts ist Siegfried auf den Schlips getreten mit seiner abfälligen Bemerkung.
Ernst stepped on Siegfried's toes with his snide remark.

auf Zack sein

to be on the ball
Meine Oma ist zwar alt, aber noch ganz schön auf Zack.
My grandma may be old, but she's still on the ball.

gewieft sein

to be street smart
Heinrich hat zwar keinen Abschluss, aber ist ganz schön gewieft.
Heinrich might not have a diploma, but he's street smart.

Konkurrent, m.

competitor, rival

**Adidas und Puma sind seit Jahrzehnten starke Konkur-
renten im Sportartikelbereich.**
*When it comes to sports gear, Adidas and Puma have been strong
competitors for decades.*

den Bach runter gehen
to go down the drain; lit. to go down the creek
Unsere Aktien gehen den Bach runter.
Our stocks are going down the drain.

Feierabend, m.
closing time, leisure time
**Willst du nach Feierabend mit mir ein Bier trinken
gehen?**
Do you want to grab a beer with me after work?

*At the end of the work day, German co-workers wish
each other* einen schönen Feierabend, *which is much
nicer than our "Have a good night," since* Feierabend
(feiern—to celebrate; Abend—evening) *better reflects
the celebratory "high" you experience at the close of
another work day. By the way, the* Feierabend Bier *is the
best pint you can possibly have.*

den Hut nehmen müssen
to pack one's bags; lit. must take the hat
**Der Meier wird wohl seinen Hut nehmen müssen. Die wol-
len seine Stelle abbauen.**
Meier will have to pack his bags. They want to phase out his job.

ein Schlag ins Wasser
flop; lit. a blow in the water
Ihr Konzert war ein Schlag ins Wasser. Nur eine Handvoll Leute kamen, um sie zu hören.
Their concert was a flop. Only a handful of people showed up to hear them.

Büromief, m.
dreary, depressing office atmosphere; lit. stale office air
Ich muss dringend raus aus diesem Büromief.
I have to get out of this depressing office atmosphere.

kostbar wie Beamtenschweiß
something very rare and precious; lit. as precious as the sweat of a government worker
Ein Sonnentag im April in Deutschland ist so kostbar wie Beamtenschweiß.
A sunny April day in Germany is a rare and precious thing.
Lit. A sunny April day in Germany is as precious as the sweat of a government worker.

Paragraphenreiter, m.
stickler for the rules; lit. a paragraph rider
Niemand im Büro mag den Karl, aber er ist selbst Schuld daran. Was muss er auch so'n Paragraphenreiter sein.
No one in the office likes Karl, but it's his own fault. He doesn't have to be such a stickler for rules.

Amtsschimmel, m.
red tape; lit. bureaucratic white horse
Der Amtsschimmel wiehert!
The red tape never ends!
The bureaucratic white horse whinnies!

Tippse, f.

secretary, typist

In meinem Job werde ich wie'ne bessere Tippse behandelt. So habe ich mir Marketing nicht vorgestellt.

In my job I'm treated like a well paid typist. That's not how I imagined marketing would be.

This term comes straight from card player lingo, where players can cheat by hiding good cards in their sleeves and secretly shake them out of their sleeves when needed.

Ärmel hochkrempeln

to roll up one's sleeves

Ok Jungs, jetzt heißt's Ärmel hochkrempeln und ran an die Arbeit!

Ok people, let's roll up our sleeves and get to work!

CHAPTER TEN

Geldsucht und bargeldlos:

Shake Your Moneymaker

Traveler's checks may not be commonplace anymore, but it may surprise you that traveling around Germany with only plastic can be less than fantastic. While the number of shops that accept this form of payment has climbed in recent years, the fear of identity theft and deep personal debt scares the Germans. With the average American carrying more than a dozen credit cards—and around $10,000 in debt—our frugal friends have decided to avoid them like the plague.

As a result, only one quarter of Germans carry a credit card. Best to buy only what you can afford now, they say, and if they do use plastic, they pay their balance in full each month. In other words, by American standards, Germans are cheap. People start stashing away their *Notgroschen*, or "nest egg," before they can drive and preparing their pensions before their first grey hair appears. They say "*Geiz ist geil*", so don't forget that rather than being frowned upon, "Stingy is cool." While the Dutch normally get all the attention in this area, note that there is only a two-letter difference between Dutch and *Deutsch* . . .

Fuffi, m.

fifty euro bill, from *fünfzig*

He, wann krieg ich denn den Fuffi zurück, den du letzte Woche geliehen hast?

Hey, when will I get back my fifty euro bill that you borrowed last week?

Hunni, m.

hundred euro bill, from *hundert*

Die Turnschuhe haben mich fast 'nen Hunni gekostet!

The sneakers cost me almost a hundred euros!

Zwanni, m.

twenty euro bill, from *zwanzig*

Die haben mich gerippt, aber zum Glück hatte ich nur für'n Zwanni was dabei.

I got jumped, but luckily I only had stuff worth twenty euros on me.

pumpen

to borrow; lit. to pump

Vati, darf ich mir bei dir was pumpen?

Dad, can I borrow some cash from you?

Mäuse, pl

cash; lit. mice

Das sind 'ne Menge Mäuse.

That's a whole lot of cash.

Schotter, m.

money; lit. ballast

Führ mich zum Schotter!

Show me the money!

73

Knete, f.
dough
Nu schieb' die Knete schon rüber, du Geizhals!
Just fork over the dough, you tightwad!

Zaster, Mäuse und Moneten—*dough, moolah, and smackeroos*

Wouldn't it be fabulous to change Heu *(hay)*, Kies *(gravel)*, or Kohle *(coal)* into cold, hard cash? We'd like to score some Asche *(ash)* and make some gold from Pulver *(powder)* and Flocken *(flakes)*. How nice if we could change Flöhe *(fleas)*, Moos *(moss)*, and Kröten *(toads)* into small change and bills. Why are there so many terms? Because: Ohne Moos nix los! *No money, no fun.*

blank sein
to be broke; lit. to be bare
Ich bin total blank.
I'm flat broke.

Ebbe, f.
low, at an ebb
In meinem Geldbeutel herrscht Ebbe.
My finances are at an ebb.

ergeiern
to buy at a flea market or yard sale; from *Geier*, vulture
Der Erik hat sich seine gesamte Einrichtung auf Flohmärkten ergeiert.
Erik bought all his furniture at flea markets.

Notgroschen, m.

rainy day fund; lit. emergency penny

Ich möchte meinen Notgroschen nicht für einen Urlaub ausgeben.

I don't want to spend my rainy day fund on a vacation.

Reibach machen

to profit; from the Yiddish word *rewach*, to profit

Mit dem Verkauf seines Geschäfts hat mein Vater einen großen Reibach gemacht.

My father made a big profit by selling his store.

bar auf die Kralle

cash in one's hand; lit. cash on the claw

Ich will mein Geld bar auf die Kralle oder es gibt Stunk!

I want the cash in my hands or else there'll be trouble!

Haufen Geld, m.

an arm and a leg; lit. heap of money

Das neue Handy hat Lola einen Haufen Geld gekostet.

Lola's new cell phone cost her an arm and a leg.

Einem Geld aus der Tasche ziehen

to squeeze money out of someone, to rob someone blind; lit. to take money from someone's pockets

Schon wieder eine Telefonrechnung. Die ziehen einem wirklich das Geld aus der Tasche.

Here we go, another phone bill. I tell you they're robbing us blind.

für Umme

for free, from *umsonst*

Nix ist für Umme!

Nothing in life is free!

Vermögen, n.
fortune
Der Urlaub hat uns ein Vermögen gekostet, aber er war's wert.
The vacation cost us a fortune, but it was worth it.

Geld verplempern
to waste money
Mensch, der Kinofilm war bescheuert, da haben wir unser Geld umsonst verplempert.
Man, that movie was a flop, what a total waste of our money.

verbraten
to fritter away or blow money; lit. to overcook
Den Lohn von meinem Sommerjob habe ich schon an Spielautomaten verbraten.
I've already blown the money I made from my summer job on video games.

pleite sein
to be down-and-out, broke, bankrupt
Wenn man pleite ist, dann zeigen sich die wahren Freunde.
When you are down-and-out, you learn who your real friends are.

knapp bei Kasse sein
to be strapped for cash
Das neue Handy kann ich vergessen. Ich bin im Moment knapp bei Kasse.
I can forget about the new cell phone. I'm strapped for cash at the moment.

Durststrecke, f.
hard times, dry spell; lit. a thirsty stretch

Nach einer Durststrecke klettern unsere Aktien endlich wieder ein wenig.
After a dry spell, our stocks are finally rising a little bit again.

blechen
to fork out or shell out money
Du hast den Schaden eingebrockt, also kannst du dafür auch blechen.
You got us into this trouble, now fork over the money to get us out of it.

Geld verjubeln
to splurge, blow money
Du kannst dir doch diesen neuen BMW nicht leisten! Da hast du eine Menge Geld verjubelt.
You can't afford this new BMW! You just blew a lot of money.

sich eine goldene Nase verdienen
to make a killing; lit. to earn oneself a golden nose
Mit seiner Erfindung hat Gerhardt sich eine goldene Nase verdient.
Gerhardt made a killing on his invention.

bei jemandem tief in der Kreide stehen
to be deep in debt to someone
Er steht bei seinen Freunden tief in der Kreide.
He's deep in debt to his friends.

den Geldhahn zudrehen
to stop providing money, to cut off funds; lit. to turn off the money faucet
Nach meiner fünf in Mathe haben mir meine Eltern den Geldhahn zugedreht.
After I got an F in math, my parents cut off my monthly allowance.

arm dran sein
to be badly off, in a bad situation
Claudia ist wirklich arm dran: Der Carlo hat ihr Konto
geplündert und ist einfach abgehauen.
Claudia is badly off: Carlo looted her account and just took off.

Schnäppchen, n.
steal, deal, bargain
Der reduzierte Hugo Boss Anzug im Schaufenster ist ein
echtes Schnäppchen.
The Hugo Boss suit on sale in the window is a steal.

Schnäppchenjäger, m.
bargain hunter
Meine Freundin und ich sind echte Schnäppchenjäger. Wir
wissen über jeden Schlussverkauf Bescheid.
My friend and I are real bargain hunters. We know about every
sale.

klamm sein
broke; lit. clammy
Ich bin klamm.
I'm broke.

voll Aldi, aldig
dirt cheap, good value; from the bargain-basement German supermarket chain *Aldi*
Das HDTV-Gerät für nur 499 Euro ist ja aldig.
The HDTV for only 499 euros is dirt cheap.

CHAPTER ELEVEN

Oberinspektor Derrick:

The Wrong Side of the Law

Anyone who's seen a World War II movie has heard the phrase "Zese paperz are not in orter." Even today, Germans aged sixteen and older are obligated to carry an ID with them or face detainment until their identity is verfied. But it is not enough to be wary of the police—in Germany and the German-speaking area of Switzerland, your neighbors are the greatest threat to your freedom. That's right, even at home one must behave in a civilized manner. This means no loud noise after a certain time, usually 8 or 10 P.M., or before 8 A.M., excluding Sundays and holidays. In Switzerland this is taken one step further, and in many apartment buildings, even flushing the toilet or making love after "lights out" time can be a criminal activity. Sundays and holidays mean even more restrictions—unless you want to live like the *Assos* (notice it sounds strangely like assholes), lit. asocials or "white trash," you'll act like you're ten years old again at sleep away camp and do as the counselor says, "Shhhhhhhhh!"

Tobacco and Other Drugs

kiffen
to toke
Reich mal den Joint, ich möchte kiffen.
Pass that joint, I want to toke.

jamaikanische Luft reichen
to smell weed, to smell Jamaican air
Ey, riech mal . . . jamaikanische Luft!
Hey, take a whiff . . . weed!

knülle sein
to be stoned
Ey Alter, bin ich wieder knülle!
S'up, I'm stoned man!

Fluppe, f.
cigarette
Komm, gib mir mal ne Fluppe.
Come on, give me a cigarette.

Kung-Fu Puder, n.
coke; lit. kung fu powder
Wow, echt Superwahnsinn, dein Kung-Fu Puder.
Wow, your coke is far out.

spliffen
to smoke weed
Jo, ich geb einen aus, eine Runde spliffen für alle.
Yo, my treat, one round of weed for everyone.

straff sein
to be loaded

Nachdem Peter die Wasserpfeife geraucht hatte, war er so straff, dass er nicht mehr gerade laufen konnte.
After smoking the bong, Peter was so loaded that he couldn't walk straight.

suchten
to get hooked; lit. to addict, from *die Sucht*, addiction
Suchte mal nicht an den Kippen, ist ja unmöglich.
Don't get hooked on cigarettes—it's ridiculous.

Kristaller, m.
crankster, speed freak
Am Bahnhof hat so ein Kristaller 'ne Oma überfallen.
At the train station some crankster jumped an old lady.

Ticket, n.
acid; lit. ticket
Letzte Woche bin ich im Tanzschuppen gewesen, hab ich mir'n Ticket andrehen lassen.
Last week I went to the disco and someone talked me into trying acid.

Tüte, f.
joint; lit. bag
Ich werde eine Tüte rauchen und einfach nur relaxen.
I'm going to smoke a joint and just chill.

verballert
under the influence, wasted; lit. squandered
Mann Günther, du siehst ja mal völlig verballert aus. Du kannst nicht mehr nach Hause fahren.
Geez, Günther, you look totally wasted. You can't drive home.

total verstrahlt sein
to be high as a kite; lit. to be radiated
Am Wochenende hab ich vielleicht was geraucht, sag ich di, ich war total verstrahlt.
I smoked so much on the weekend, I tell you, I was high as a kite.

vollgequarzt sein
to be completely high
Mann, ist der vollgequarzt.
Man, he's completely high.

sich zudröhnen
to get stoned, wasted
Ich dröhn mich heute Abend mal zu, sonst ertrag ich den ganzen Scheiß nicht mehr.
I'm going to get wasted tonight, otherwise I can't take this bullshit anymore.

Ticker, m.
dealer; lit. ticker
Ich bin wieder knapp dran, muss mich bald mal wieder mit meinem Ticker treffen.
My stash is low. I gotta meet up with my dealer again soon.

Gärtner, m.
dealer; lit. gardener
Petra hat nichts mehr zu rauchen da und muss erst wieder zu ihrem Gärtner.
Petra doesn't have anything left to smoke and has to see her dealer.

Zoff, m.
trouble

Mach hier keinen Zoff!
Don't make any trouble here!

Bulle, m.
cop
Dieter kann's nicht glauben, dass deine Freundin ein Bulle ist.
Dieter can't believe your girlfriend is a cop.

Männer in Grün, pl.
boys in blue; lit. men in green
Obacht, Manni! Hier kommen die Männer in Grün.
Watch it, Manni! Here come the boys in blue.

Polente, f.
cops
Die Polente ist manchmal zu übereifrig im Gesetzesvollzug.
Cops are sometimes overzealous in their enforcement of the law.

klatschen
to beat up; lit. to clap
Geh nicht zu dem Klub. Mein Freund wurde dort geklatscht.
Don't go to that club. My friend got beat up there.

abzocken
to rip off
Zehn Dollar für ein Bier? Die zocken einen hier ganz schön ab.
Ten dollars for a beer? This place is a total rip off.

Abzocker, m.
hustler
Lass dich nicht auf den Kerl ein; er ist der totale Abzocker.
Don't get involved with that guy; he's a real hustler.

Rauferei, f.
brawl
Hast du von der Rauferei nach dem Fußballspiel gehört?
Did you hear about the brawl after the football game?

Handgemenge, n.
melee; lit. hand mixture

Ja, es gab ein Handgemenge nach dem anderen.
Yes, there was one melee after another.

Klopperei, f.
alley fight
Der Boxkampf sah eher nach einer Klopperei aus.
The boxing match looked more like an alley fight.

Bösewicht, m.
badass, the bad guy; lit. mean midget
Mein schwester glaubt, sie sei ein Bösewicht, aber in Wahrheit ist sie viel braver.
My sister thinks she's a badass, but she's really a softie.

Schurke, m.
villain
Der Schurke ist uns entwischt.
The villain slipped away.

jemanden verpfeifen
to squeal on somebody; lit. to blow the whistle on someone
Atze hat Ali bei der Polizei verpfiffen.
Atze squealed on Ali to the police.

mit der Polizei Versteck spielen
to dodge the police; lit. to play hide-and-seek with the police

Der Ganove rannte durch enge Gassen und Hinterhöfe und spielte mit der Polizei Versteck.
The crook went down narrow alleyways and backyards to dodge the cops.

dümmer sein als die Polizei erlaubt

to be as stupid as they come; lit. to be dumber than the police allow

Wenn du glaubst, du kannst mich fertigmachen, dann bist du dümmer als die Polizei erlaubt.

If you think you can torment me, than you are as stupid as they come.

jemandem dicht auf den Fersen sein

to be right on someone's heels

Wiley Coyote ist dem Roadrunner immer dicht auf den Fersen, aber er kann ihn nie fangen.

Wiley Coyote is always right on Roadrunner's heels, but he can never catch him.

bei jemandem in Ungnade sein

to be in the doghouse with someone

Ich bin nach Mitternacht betrunken nach Hause gekommen und bin jetzt bei meinen Mitbewohnern in Ungnade.

I came home drunk after midnight and now I'm really in the doghouse with my roommates.

mit jemandem in Konflikt geraten

to have a run-in with someone

Das Letzte was ich wollte war mit dem Muskelprotz in Konflikt zu geraten.

The last thing I wanted to do is have a run-in with that huge guy.

nichts Gutes verheißen

to spell trouble; lit. to foretell nothing good

Boris' Gesichtsausdruck verhieß nichts Gutes. Und schon blitzte auch eine Klinge in seiner Hand.

Boris' expression spelled trouble, and then he had a knife in his hand.

sich jemanden schnappen

to arrest someone

Die Bullen waren nicht sicher wen, aber sie wollten ganz sicher jemanden schnappen.

The cops weren't sure whom, but they definitely wanted to arrest somebody.

beim Wickel fassen

to collar

Die Bullen fassten den Dieb beim Wickel.

The cops collared the thief.

Schlitzohr, n.

crook, sly dog; lit. slit-ear

Deine Schwester ist ein gewieftes Schlitzohr.

Your sister is a sly dog.

mit allen Wassern gewaschen sein

to know all the tricks in the book; lit. to be washed with all waters

Wirklich gute Diebe, die mit allen Wassern gewaschen sind, lassen sich nicht fangen.

Really good thieves, who know all the tricks in the book, don't let themselves get caught.

jemanden ablinken

to deceive someone

Helmut konnte alle ablinken und wurde nie gefasst.
Helmut could deceive everyone and never get caught.

absahnen
to hit the gravy train; lit. to skim off the cream
Peter hat als Kredithai ganz groß abgesahnt.
Peter hit the gravy train as a loan shark.

jemandem das Handwerk legen
to put a stop to someone's game
Dieser Kerl ist ein gemeiner Betrüger. Man sollte ihm das Handwerk legen.
This guy is a low-life cheater. Someone has to put a stop to his game.

Similarly, jemandem in den Sack stecken—*lit. to put someone in the sack—is closest to the American expression "to knock someone's socks off." It comes from the popular sport of jousting. In the Middle Ages, the loser of a tournament was squeezed into a sack and dragged by the winner's horse.*

Abschaum, m.
scum
Die Typen mit denen du abhängst sind der Abschaum der menschlichen Gesellschaft.
The losers you're hanging out with are the scum of the earth.

eintüten
to steal; lit. to bag

Emmanuel wusste nicht, wie man sein Geld ehrlich
verdient, aber er wusste genau, wie man sich etwas
eintütet.
*Emmanuel didn't know how to earn money honestly, but he did
know how to steal.*

Fünf-Finger-Rabatt, m.

to steal; lit. five-finger discount
Ich kann mir das Hemd nicht leisten, es sei denn ich be-
nutze den Fünf-Finger-Rabatt.
I can't afford that shirt unless I use the five-finger discount.

zecken

to pilfer or steal something, from *Zecke*, tick
Boa, mir haben sie gestern zum dritten Mal dieses Jahr
mein Fahrrad gezeckt!
Damn, yesterday my bike got stolen for the third time this year!

etwas moppsen

to pinch something
Ich hab heut in der Drogerie einfach einen Nagellack
gemoppst.
Today in the drugstore I just pinched some nail polish.

einklaufen gehen

to go shoplifting, from *einkaufen*, to shop, and *klauen*, to steal
He, ich brauche mal wieder neue CDs, lass uns irgendwo
einklaufen gehen. Ich bin nämlich blank.
Hey, I need new CDs, let's go shoplifting. I'm broke.

jemandem den Garaus machen

to finish somebody off

Das Opfer war zunächst nur verletzt, aber dann machte ihm der Mörder den Garaus.
The victim was only wounded at first, but then the killer finished him off.

abmurksen

to kill

Nur ein eiskaltes Herz kann jemanden abmurksen.
It takes a cold heart to kill.

When mobsters kill, they don't usually want others to hear about their plans. To achieve this, they have developed clever euphemisms for the verb "to kill." Often a vicitm will be brought just around the corner (of a cliff), jemanden um die Ecke bringen, *or will be* beseitigt, *set on the side (of a long pier). In cold blood, other criminals will just* kaltmachen, *cool off,* neutralisieren, *neutralize, or* terminieren, *terminate, the life of their* Opfer, *or victim.*

CHAPTER TWELVE

Alles hat ein Ende, nur die Wurst hat zwei:
Following Doctors' Orders

Health is certainly one of the more serious, but also one of the most popular topics for Germans. You might have never worried about *Kreislaufstörung*—lit. circulatory collapse—high blood pressure, or your cholesterol level, but you will in *Deutschland*. Germans are decidedly robust and healthy in general, but the suspicious ailments they develop may not ring a bell with you. *Kreislaufstörung* is quite a phenomenon; while circulatory collapse sounds life-threatening, this illness is slightly less acute. Sufferers stay home and rest, which is naturally the only cure.

Even worse, things you once considered harmless are suddenly very dangerous in German-speaking nations. A gust of wind or a draft can be deadly, so if you hear *Es zieht!*, close the window immediately or run for cover. In Switzerland and Austria, the *Föhn* is responsible for thousands of sick days each year. This warm northerly wind from Africa is blamed for a whole host of disorders, including the flu, headaches, nausea, and even strange behavior. They may sound alike, but for most of these German speakers, the *Föhn* is no fun.

Where to Go When You're Ill

Hausarzt, Hausärztin m./f.
GP, lit. house doctor
Mein Hausarzt kennt mich, seitdem ich ein Kind war.
My GP has known me since I was a kid.

Kariesverwalter, m.
dentist; lit. cavity administrator
Ich muss morgen zum Kariesverwalter. Hoffentlich bohrt er nicht.
I have to go to the dentist tomorrow. Hopefully he won't drill.

Elfenbeinchirug, m.
dentist; lit. ivory surgeon
Kannst du mir einen guten Elfenbeinchirurg empfehlen?
Can you recommend a good dentist?

Halbgötter in Weiß, pl.
doctors; lit. demigods in white
Die Halbgötter in Weiß sind total eingebildet.
These doctors are totally full of themselves.

Seelenklempner, m.
shrink; lit. soul plumber
Siegmar sollte einen Seelenklempner aufsuchen. Er ist immer so deprimiert.
Siegmar should get a shrink. He's always so depressed.

Höhlenforscher, m.
gyno; lit. cave explorer

Hab gestern mit so 'nem Typen gepennt und mir irgendwas eingefangen. Ich glaub, ich muss mal zum Höhlenforscher.
Yesterday I slept with some dude and caught something. I ought to see the gynecologist.

Kurpfuscher, m.
quack, lit. spa botcher
Sie sind ein ganz mieser Kurpfuscher!
You're just a two-bit quack!

Frühjahrsmüdigkeit, f.
spring fever; lit. spring fatigue
Wenn man sich im Frühling nur schwer konzentrieren kann, leiden Deutsche unter sogenannter Frühjahrsmüdigkeit.
When it's hard to concentrate in spring, many Germans blame spring fever.

sich beschissen fühlen
to feel like crap
Ich fühle mich beschissen. Ich glaube ich geh sofort ins Bett.
I feel like crap. I think I'm going straight to bed.

speiübel sein
to be sick to your stomach
Ich fühle mich nicht so gut, mir ist speiübel.
I don't feel well, I feel sick to my stomach.

sterbenskrank
deathly ill (used only in the humorous sense)
Mein Mann ist bei jedem kleinen Schnupfen sterbenskrank!
My husband thinks he's deathly ill whenever he gets a little cold!

Eine gesunde Verdorbenheit ist besser als 'ne verdorbene Gesundheit–A Healthy Rottenness is Better than Rotten Health

ins Gras beißen
to bite the dust; lit. to bite the grass
Bevor ich ins Gras beiße, möcht ich noch 'n bisschen Spaß haben.
Before I bite the dust, I want to have a little fun.

sich abmelden
to die; lit. to sign off
Wenn du weiterhin so viel qualmst, kannst du dich bald abmelden.
If you keep smoking like this, you'll die soon.

den Löffel abgeben
to kick the bucket; lit. to give up the spoon
Hat der alte Knacker jetzt endlich den Löffel abgegeben?
Did the old geezer finally kick the bucket?

die Augen auf Null stellen
to die, to be toast; lit. to set the eyes to zero
Noch so 'ne Bemerkung und ich stelle dir die Augen auf Null.
One more snide remark from you and you're toast.

die Radieschen von unten betrachten
pushing the daisies; lit. to watch the radishes from below
Onkel Ottmar kann jetzt die Radieschen von unten betrachten. Zumindest musste er nicht lange leiden.
Uncle Ottmar is pushing daisies now. At least he didn't suffer long.

Holzmantel, m.

coffin; lit. wooden coat

Der Nachbar vom Schmidt trägt schon seit einem Jahr einen Holzmantel.

Schmidt's neighbor's been dead for a year now.

Lit. Schmidt's neighbor's been wearing a wooden coat for a year now.

Births

jemanden dick machen

to knock someone up; lit. to make someone fat

Andrea wurde von ihrem Ex dick gemacht, aber sie kann ihn nicht mehr leiden.

Andrea got knocked up by her ex, but she can't stand him anymore.

einen Braten in der Röhre haben

to have a bun in the oven; lit. to have a roast in the oven

Silke hat einen Braten in der Röhre.

Silke has a bun in the oven.

in anderen Umständen sein

to be pregnant; lit. to be in different circumstances

Haben Sie schon gehört? Die Tochter von Frau Klarsen ist in anderen Umständen.

Have you heard? Frau Klarsen's daughter is pregnant.

vom Storch gebissen

pregnant; lit. to be bitten by the stork

Mara wurde vom Storch ins Bein gebissen.

Mara is pregnant.

die Pille nehmen
to take the pill
Patricia nimmt seit drei Monaten die Pille.
Patricia has been taking the pill for three months now.

Wehwehchen, n.
boo-boo
Bei jedem kleinen Wehwehchen heulst du.
Every little boo-boo makes you cry.

vor Schmerzen sterben
to die of pain
Tu doch nicht so als würdest du vor Schmerzen sterben. Ist doch nur eine ganz kleine Wunde.
Don't pretend you're dying of pain. It's just a little cut.

sich den Tripper holen
to get a dose of the clap
Wenn du dich mit der einlässt, holst du dir garantiert den Tripper.
If you mess with her you'll get a dose of the clap for sure.

Sackratte, f.
crabs, pubic lice; lit. pubic rat
Nachdem er mit Sophie ins Bett gestiegen war, hat Uwe sich Sackratten geholt.
After he climbed into bed with Sophie, Uwe ended up with a case of the crabs.

CHAPTER THIRTEEN

Krieg und Frieden:

Looking for Trouble and Keeping the Peace

Germany is a land of contradictions. While responsible for two World Wars, Germans also hold the world's largest annual peace celebration. In order to redeem themselves after 1945, it seems they have taken the motto, "Make love, not war" to heart. *Love-parade* is a techno dance street festival whose revelers border on insanity . . . think the flamboyance of San Francisco's Castro district Halloween parade meets the drunkenness of Chicago's St. Patrick's Day parade. The event is hosted by a different city every year.

But it's not all lovey-dovey. In general, fights are surprisingly few and far between in Germany, but when they occur, watch out. If you are a person of color, there are certain areas in Berlin and other formerly East-German cities that should be avoided, especially at night. In recent years, neo-Nazism has been on the rise, but with few Jews left to blame, these national socialists pick on those of Turkish and Indian descent. Despite this fact, it remains illegal to display a *Swastika* in any form, or to possess Hitler's infamous *Mein Kampf*. If only the black leather chaps worn at *Loveparade* had the same status . . .

Annoyances

Streit suchen
to look for trouble
Manche Jugendliche suchen den Streit förmlich.
Some teenage boys are genuinely looking for trouble.

Unannehmlichkeiten herausfordern
to provoke
Du hast eine Art immer Unannehmlichkeiten herauszufordern.
You have a way of always provoking people.

jemanden anstarren
to stare at someone
Der Kerl in der U-Bahn hat mich ununterbrochen angestarrt.
This guy on the subway just kept staring at me.

Do you have a booger hanging out of your nose, or is your fly down? Nope, that German (staring occurs to a lesser degree in Austria and ever-polite Switzerland) is just staring at you for no apparent reason. Staring could even be considered a national pastime here, as the number of hours devoted to ogling others is comparable to the hours spent watching Fussball. *What can you do? One solution is to wear sunglasses with mirror lenses. The other is to get used to it.*

blickficken
to ogle, to undress with one's eyes; lit. to look-f**k
Lass' uns heute Abend mal in die Stadt ein bisschen blick-ficken gehen.
Let's go out tonight and ogle some chicks.

jemanden auf den Sack/den Keks gehen
to get on someone's nerves; lit. to get on someone's scrotum/cookie
Hör mit dem Geschrei auf. Das geht mir total auf den Sack.
Just stop that yelling. You're getting on my nerves.

Affenspektakel, n.
brouhaha; lit. monkey spectacle
Was soll das Affenspektakel?
What's all this brouhaha?

jemanden den Buckel runterrutschen
to want someone to get lost; lit. to slide down someone's hump
Rutsch mir den Buckel 'runter!
Get lost!

die Nase voll haben von jemandem
to have it up to here with someone; lit. to have the nose full of someone
Die ganze Nacht hast du mich schon so doof angemacht, jetzt habe ich aber die Nase voll von dir.
You've been bothering me all night and now I've had it up to here with you.

sich kabbeln
to squabble, to bicker with someone
Den Karl kannst du nicht zur Party einladen. Der kabbelt sich mit jedem.

You can't invite Karl to the party. He bickers with everybody.

angriffslustig
aggressive, belligerent
Einige Typen von meiner Schule sind total angriffslustig.
Some kids at my school are extremely belligerent.

wegen jeder Kleinigkeit streiten
to quarrel; lit. to fight about every little thing
Warum müssen wir uns eigentlich immer wegen jeder Kleinigkeit streiten?
Why do we have to quarrel all the time?

fetzen
to argue
Mensch, guck mal, wie sich Klaus und Barbara wieder fetzen.
Look, Klaus and Barbara are arguing again.

(an)motzen
to scold,to swear at somebody
Während der Auseinandersetzung hat Jeff seinen Bruder angemotzt.
Jeff swore at his brother during the argument.

Egotrip, m.
ego trip
Du bist mal wieder total auf dem Egotrip.
You're on a total ego trip again!

zoffen
to fight
Hör mal, ich möchte mich nicht mit Dir zoffen.
Look, I don't want to fight with you.

sich verpissen

to piss off

Verpiss dich, sonst knallt's!

Piss off or I'll sock it to you!

Leine ziehen

to get lost; lit. to pull the line

Zieh Leine, wenn Du nicht die Fresse poliert bekommen willst.

Get lost if you don't want a good beating.

Terz haben

to argue, to have an altercation

Mein Nachbar und ich haben Terz, weil er nie seinen Müll aufhebt.

My neighbor and I have an altercation because he never picks up his garbage.

Fratzengeballer, n.

hit in the face

Pass auf, was du sagst, sonst gibt's hier gleich Fratzengeballer!

Watch what you say if you don't want to get hit in the face!

abmischen

to give somebody a thrashing, to mix someone up

Er war der Unterlegene, aber er konnte den anderen ganz gut abmischen.

He was the underdog, but he gave the other guy a good thrashing.

jemanden abbürsten

to beat someone; lit. to brush someone

Nachdem die Heimmannschaft verloren hatte, wollten die Fans einfach nur jemanden ordentlich abbürsten.

After the home team lost the game, the team's fans were just looking to beat someone.

(sich) eine fangen
to get a slap; lit. to catch one
Fass sie nicht untenrum an, oder du fängst dir eine.
Don't touch her down there or you'll get a slap.

Backpfeife, f.
slap; lit. cheek whistle
Nach der Backpfeife war sein Gesicht noch 'ne halbe Stunde rot.
After the slap, his face stayed red for half an hour.

Backpfeifengesicht, n.
face that cries out for a fist in it; lit. cheek whistle face
Du kennst den Typ, er hat das totale Backpfeifengesicht.
You know the type, he has a face that cries out for a fist in it.

jemandem den Buckel vollhauen
to give somebody a good beating
Dem Fahrraddieb habe ich ordentlich den Buckel vollgehauen.
I gave the bicycle thief a good beating.

sich jemanden (ordentlich) vorknöpfen
to give somebody a good talking to
Als sie um 2 Uhr morgens zu Hause auftauchte, hat ihre Mutter sie sich aber erstmal ordentlich vorgeknöpft.
When she showed up at home at 2 a.m., her mother gave her a good talking to.

sich mit jemandem anlegen
to mess with somebody

Der Typ ist hartgesotten. Ich glaube nicht, dass du dich mit ihm anlegen willst.

He's a very tough guy. I don't think you want to mess with him.

sich mit jemandem verkrachen

to have a falling out with somebody

Mein Cousin war immer mein bester Freund, aber nach unserer Meinungsverschiedenheit haben wir uns total verkracht.

My cousin used to be my best friend but after our argument we had a complete falling out.

sich um Kopf und Kragen reden

to risk one's neck with careless talk; lit. to risk head and collar through talking

Du musst lernen diplomatischer zu sein. Du hast uns fast um Kopf und Kragen geredet.

You have to learn to be more diplomatic. You almost risked our necks with your careless talk.

jemandem die Fresse polieren

to hit someone in the face; lit. to polish someone's mouth

Als Louise sagte ihm gehört die Fresse poliert, meinte sie nicht mit Lippenstift.

When Louise said he should have his mouth polished, she didn't mean with lipstick.

sich in die Haare kriegen

to get into each other's hair

Kriegt euch mal nicht in die Haare! Peace, Brüder!

Don't get into each other's hair! Peace, brothers!

sich mit jemandem kloppen

to fight with someone

Er ist besoffen und wartet nur darauf, sich mit jemandem zu kloppen.
He's drunk and he's just dying to fight with someone.

einen Streit vom Zaun brechen
to pick a fight; lit. to break a fight off the fence
Es gibt wirklich keinen Grund einen Streit vom Zaun zu brechen.
There's really no reason to pick a fight.

runterkommen
to calm down; lit. to come down
Komm mal wieder runter!
Calm down!

Friede, Freude, Eierkuchen
hunky-dory; lit. peace, joy, pancake
Vorhin haben sie sich noch gestritten, aber nun ist alles wieder Friede, Freude, Eierkuchen.
A while ago they were fighting, but now everything is hunky-dory again.

sich verdünnisieren
to get out of here; lit. to do a vanishing trick
Sobald das Bier alle ist, werde ich mich verdünnisieren.
As soon as the beer is gone, I'm out of here.

sich drücken
to chicken out, to get out of doing something
Wir wollten sky-diven, aber im letzten Moment haben wir uns davor gedrückt.
We were going to sky dive, but we chickened out at the last minute.

sich wegscheren

to clear off

Die Anhänger sind auf das Spielfeld gerannt, aber ihnen wurde gesagt, sie sollen sich wegscheren.

The fans ran onto the field but they were ordered to clear off.

sich dünne machen

to make oneself scarce; lit. to make oneself thin

Wenn du weißt, was für dich gut ist, dann wirst du dich dünne machen.

If you know what's good for you, you'll make yourself scarce.

sich aus dem Staub machen

to fly the coop; lit. to leave the dust

Sie haben seine Wohnung nach ihm durchsucht, aber er hatte sich bereits aus dem Staub gemacht.

They looked for him at home, but he had already flown the coop.

die Fliege machen

to run away, to disappear; lit. to make a fly

Der Lehrer hat den aufmüpfigen Schüler aufgefordert 'ne Fliege zu machen.

The teacher told the bratty student to get lost.

FIRST CLASS

CHAPTER FOURTEEN

Heil Geil!:

Life is a Cabaret, Beer Garden, or Disco

Gracing nearly every block, sex shops and cinemas are second only to kebab stands in Germany. For some kicks, sit at a café during lunchtime and watch the customers go in and out of an adult establishment. You'll see every *Hinz und Kunz*, from grubby old drunks to well-dressed businessmen, enter to catch a quick porn flick. Sex shops are found in the most mundane places, from malls to main streets, and even in Frankfurt International Airport. Who says airports are boring? Here, one of the first sights to greet international travelers is enormous vibrators and cock rings on display in a sex shop window. And they say Germans don't know how to have a good time.

When stepping out on the town, be forewarned of the difference between a *Nightclub* and a *Disco*. The *Disco* isn't your mother's 1970s roller derby hangout, but rather a hip, youth-packed club pulsating with ear-blasting techno music. The *Nightclub*, on the other hand, can be a much less savory experience—unless naked women picking up euro bills (and not with their hands) are your thing.

Freudenhaus, n.
brothel; lit. pleasure house
Hast Du schon mal ein Freudenhaus besucht?
Have you ever been to a brothel?

If you are walking down an average street in Nurem-berg or Wiesbaden, you may wish to talk to a beautiful woman you see while passing an open window. This lovely lady will soon be asking you what you want and how much you are willing to pay for it. This may all come as a surprise to the naive Ausländer, foreigner, who isn't aware that prostitution is perfectly legal throughout Germany, Switzerland, and Austria. Recently the state of Bavaria has made it against the law (more rules!) to have sex with a prostitute ohne Gummi, without a con-dom. What will the government insist on next?!

Puff, m.
bordello; lit. bang
Der Tourist war schockiert, einen Puff in aller Öffentlich-keit zu sehen.
The tourist was shocked to see a bordello right out in the open.

Hure, Nutte, f.
whore
Prostituierte wurden auch Huren genannt.
Prostitutes used to be called whores.

Dirne, f.
hooker

Die Dirne zeigte den Vorübergehenden ihr schönstes Lächeln.
The hooker flashed her prettiest smile at the passersby.

Flittchen, n.
floozy
Eine unbezahlte Nutte könnte man ein Flittchen nennen.
An unpaid hooker might be called a floozy.

Dirnenviertel, n.
red-light district
Manche jungen Männer gehen gerne ins Dirnenviertel.
Some young men love to go to the red-light district.

Bubistrich, m.
male prostitution, male red-light district; lit. little boy ("Bubi") for rent
Der Bubistrich ist meistens nur für Männer.
Male prostitution is mostly for men.

auf den Strich gehen
to hustle, to walk the streets; lit. to walk on the line
Die obdachlosen Frauen wurden gezwungen auf den Strich zu gehen, um Geld zu verdienen.
The homeless women were forced to walk the streets to earn money.

Prostitution has a long and colorful history in Germany. The world's oldest profession is indeed a legitimate career here, with prostitutes working in licensed brothels and paying taxes like any other hardworking German.

anschaffen

to turn tricks; lit. to aquire

Sie entschloss sich lieber anschaffen zu gehen, als einen normalen Job anzunehmen.

She decided to turn tricks rather than work a regular job.

Entertainment
Zicky-zacky, Zicky-zacky, Hoy, Hoy, Hoy!

vorglühen

to pre-party, have a drink to get you started, pre-game; lit. warm up your battery before starting the engine; "pre-glow"

Die Party beginnt um 10 Uhr. Komm doch vorher bei mir vorbei zum Vorglühen.

The party starts at 10 p.m. Why don't you come to my place first and we'll get warmed up?

abhotten

to rave it up

Heute Abend müssen wir anständig einen abhotten gehen.

We have to go rave it up tonight.

abgehen wien' Zäpfchen

to take off, to get cooking; lit. to go off like a suppository

Freitagnacht, die Party wird abgehen wie'n Zäpfchen. Ich freu' mich schon.

The party will get cooking Friday night. I'm already looking forward to it.

krachen lassen

to party hard

Peter: "Ist irgendwo `ne Party am Start?"
Steffen: "Ja, bei Steffi. Da müssen wir es heute mal
ordentlich krachen lassen!"
Peter: "Is there a party somewhere?"
Steffen: "Yeah, at Steffi's house. We have to party hard tonight!"

Aufrisszone, f.
disco; lit. the pick-up zone
Am Freitagabend entschlossen wir uns alle in die
Aufrisszone zu gehen.
On Friday night we all decided to go to the disco.

Fummelbunker, m.
club, disco; lit. the grope bunker
Die Disko war als Fummelbunker bekannt.
That disco was notorious for its raw quality.

(Tanz-)Schuppen, m.
club; lit. (dance) shack
Der Musikgruppe B52's würde der Tanzschuppen gefallen.
The band the B52's would probably like this club.

Zappelpalast, m.
nightclub; lit. fidget palace
Lass uns heute Abend den Zappelpalast besuchen.
Let's go to the nightclub tonight.

zappeln
to dance; lit. to fidget
Ich werde in die Disko gehen und meinen Frust
rauszappeln.
I'm going to the disco to dance my frustration away.

Pressbär, m.

bouncer; lit. push bear

Die zwei neuen Pressbären vom Moonlight Club wollten Manni am Samstag nicht reinlassen.

The two new bouncers at the Moonlight Club didn't want to let Manni in last Saturday.

Sir Curity, m.

bouncer, security personnel

Ernie zum Türsteher: "Ach, Sir Curity was hast du für'n Problem? Bin ich dir nich' fein genug?"

Ernie to the bouncer: "Sir Curity, what's your problem? I'm not good enough for you?"

Party machen

to party; lit. to make a party

Wir haben aufgehört zu arbeiten—es ist Zeit, Party zu machen.

We've finished working—now it's time to party.

Mucke, f.

music

Ich weiß nicht, was ich ohne Mucke machen würde.

I don't know what I'd do without music.

fett sein

phat, killer; lit. to be fat

Die Musik, die der DJ auflegt, ist echt fett.

The DJ's playing killer music.

weichgespült

middle-of-the-road, lame; lit. treated with softening agents.

Komm, lass uns verduften. Die Party ist nur weichgespült und die Typen sind auch nur Luschen.
Let's get out of here. The party is lame and the guys are just losers.

Tanzpeitsche, f.
dance floor hit; lit. dance whip
Der neue U2 Song wurde ganz schnell 'ne echte Tanzpeitsche.
The new song by U2 quickly became a dance-floor hit.

die Sau raus lassen
to go hog wild; lit. to let the pig out
Jetzt lassen wir mal so richtig die Sau raus in diesem Saftladen!
Let's go hog wild in this joint!

die Nacht um die Ohren schlagen
to pull an all-nighter, to party all night long; lit. to hit the night around your ears
Bis Freitagabend hat Kevin gebüffelt und dann entschieden, sich die Nacht um die Ohren zu schlagen.
Kevin studied until Friday evening and then decided to pull an all-nighter.

durchzechen
to drink and party through the night
Wir haben die ganze Nacht durchgezecht.
We were drinking and partying through the night.

abrocken
to dance, to party
Heute werden wir abrocken und so tun als sei es 1999.
Tonight we're going to party like it's 1999.

anheizen
to elate, to cheer, to electrify; lit. to heat up
Die Fans tobten vor Freude und die Stimmung im Stadion war angeheizt als das entscheidende Tor fiel.
The fans were elated and the atmosphere in the stadium was electrifying as the winning goal was scored.

reinhauen
to move; lit. to hit
Die Musik haut ganz schön rein!
The music really moves me!

Partybremse, f.
party-pooper; lit. party brake
Rolf, bring bitte nicht deine Freundin mit. Lass die Partybremse doch zu Hause.
Rolf, please don't bring your girlfriend. Leave the party-pooper at home.

tote Hose
dead; lit. dead pants
Hier auf der Party ist es tote Hose.
This party is dead.
Lit. Here at the party are dead pants.

Partylöwe, Salonlöwe, m.
party animal; lit. party lion, saloon lion
Seit letztem Jahr ist Jonah ein großer Partylöwe.
Since last year Jonah has been a big party animal.

Partyparasit, m.
gate crasher; lit. party parasite

Es gibt immer wieder Partyparasiten, die uneingeladen zu Parties erscheinen.
There are always gate crashers who show up at parties uninvited.

Schädelbier, n.

cheap beer (that'll give you a headache); lit. skull bear
Sag mal, habt ihr hier nur Schädelbier?
Hey, do you only have cheap beer here?

durchsumpfen

to get wasted; lit. to be mired
Sönke hat die ganze Nacht übelst durchgesumpft und sieht heute beschissen aus.
Sönke got wasted bad last night and looks like shit today.

versacken

to end up staying, get stuck somewhere
Bin gestern mal wieder in einer Kneipe versackt.
Yesterday I ended up staying in a bar again.

um die Häuser ziehen

to go out partying; lit. to stray around the block
Meine Clique und ich werden am Wochenende um die Häuser ziehen.
My buddies and I will go out partying on the weekend.

bis in die Puppen

all night long, until the wee hours of the morning
Auf der Party wurde feucht-fröhlich gefeiert, viel getrunken und bis in die Puppen getanzt.
The party was packed and entertaining, with lots of drinking and dancing all night long.

Time to Leave

heimwärts steuern

to head home; lit. to steer for home

Es ist schon spät. Lass uns heimwärts steuern.

It's getting late. Let's head home.

sich aufmachen

to leave, to head out

Ich muss mich aufmachen bevor der nächste Drink kommt.

I have to leave before I have one more drink.

einpacken

to leave, to wrap up

Lass uns einpacken. Wir haben genug gearbeitet.

Let's wrap this up. We've worked enough.

in die Falle gehen

to hit the hay; lit. to go into the trap

Nix da, kein Fernsehen mehr. Ihr geht in die Falle, Kinder.

No way, no more TV. You kids are hitting the hay.

sich aufs Ohr hauen

to nap, to go to bed; lit. to hit one's ear

Ich werd' mich mal für zwei Stunden auf's Ohr hauen.

I'm gonna nap for two hours.

abknacken

to sleep, from *Werner,* the popular German comic strip and movie character

Lass den Andi erst mal abknacken und weck ihn noch nicht.

Let Andi sleep for a while and don't wake him yet.

einknacken
to fall sleep, to crash
Martin ist sofort eingeknackt und hat das Ende vom Film verpasst.
Martin crashed immediately and missed the end of the movie.

pennen
to sleep
Warum must du eigentlich immer schon so früh pennen gehen?
Why do you always have to go to sleep so early?

poofen
to sleep, to go to bed
Nach dem Konzert wollte Verena nur noch nach Hause und poofen.
After the concert, Verena just wanted to get home and go to bed.

ratzen
to sleep
Ich habe gestern bis nach Mittag geratzt.
I slept 'til after noon yesterday.

CHAPTER FIFTEEN

Verbotene Früchte:
Forbidden Pleasures

Scheiße is the perhaps the most common cry of all in German. While it is nearly always translated as "shit," that does not begin to do it justice. *Scheiße* covers a wide range of expletives, from not-so-strong curse words to"damn" to stronger swear words, and even f**k. It is often used as a prefix, as in *Scheißjob* (stupid job) or *Scheißwetter* (rotten weather), or combined with adjectives. When you don't give a damn, for instance, then you'd say *"Das ist mir scheißegal."* Somebody might even tell you *"Du bist scheiße,"* which would mean that "you suck." If you are frustrated with the bad service at a restaurant or a department store, you might just call the establishment a *Scheißladen*. Interestingly, even the hippest and coolest people in German-speaking countries haven't started replacing the term *Scheiße* with English terms like (bull)shit or f**k. As a matter of fact, the German term for f**k, *ficken*, is strictly used in its sexual sense.

FKK (abbrev. Frei Körper Kultur)
nudist; lit. Free Body Culture
In Deutschland gibt es viele FKK Strände.
In Germany there are lots of nudist beaches.

FKK *or* Freikörperkultur, *lit. Free Body Culture, is the German joy of natural or nudist pleasures. The followers of this nonsexual culture are called traditional naturists,* FKK'ler, *or* Nudisten *(nudists).*

BH, m.
bra, from *Büstenhalter,* or bust-holder
Dieser "push-up" BH ist die neueste Mode.
This push-up bra is the latest fashion.

busenfrei
topless; lit. free boob
Dieser Strand war schon immer busenfrei.
This has always been a topless beach.

Oben ohne
topless
Lass uns die Oben-ohne -Tänzerinnen angucken.
Let's go and see the topless dancers.

Blitzer, m.
flasher
Ein Blitzer lief während der Halbzeit über den Fußballplatz.
A flasher ran across the soccer field during half-time.

Ekel erregend
gross; lit. disgust-generating
Pubertätspickel sind Ekel erregend.
Pimples on teenagers are gross.

Pups, m.
fart
Während des Küssens entwich Andrea ein kleiner Pups.
While kissing, Andrea let out a little fart.

Analhusten, m.
fart; lit. anal cough
Dein Analhusten ist ja brutal. Es stinkt hier wie im Gulli.
Your farts are brutal. It reeks like a sewer in here.

furzen
to fart
Wer hat gefurzt?
Who farted?

einen fahren lassen
to cut one; lit. to let one go
Er besaß die Frechheit im vollen Aufzug einen fahren zu lassen.
He had the nerve to cut one in the crowded elevator.

Flitzerkacke, f.
the runs, the shits; lit. streaking shit
Nach einer durchzechten Nacht während Karneval hat Brad die Flitzerkacke bekommen.
After a long night of partying during Carnival, Brad got the runs.

scheißen
to shit

Einer der einfachen Genüsse im Leben ist's in Ruhe zu scheißen.
One of life's simple pleasures is to shit in peace.

sanitär entspannen
to go to the bathroom; lit. sanitary relaxation
Felix wollte, glaube ich, sanitär entspannen.
I think Felix is in the bathroom.

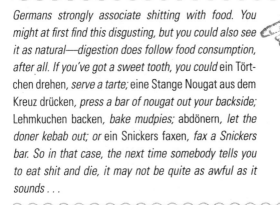

Germans strongly associate shitting with food. You might at first find this disgusting, but you could also see it as natural—digestion does follow food consumption, after all. If you've got a sweet tooth, you could ein Törtchen drehen, *serve a tarte;* eine Stange Nougat aus dem Kreuz drücken, *press a bar of nougat out your backside;* Lehmkuchen backen, *bake mudpies;* abdönern, *let the doner kebab out;* or ein Snickers faxen, *fax a Snickers bar. So in that case, the next time somebody tells you to eat shit and die, it may not be quite as awful as it sounds . . .*

(jemandem) anscheißen
to screw (someone) over
Da hast du dich aber anscheißen lassen.
You really got screwed over.

beschissen
lousy, crappy, screwed up

TALK DIRTY **GERMAN**

Wir haben die besten Pläne fürs Wochenende gemacht, aber dann hat sich Jens sein Bein gebrochen und alles war beschissen.

We made the best plans for the weekend, but then Jens broke his leg and everything got screwed up.

Arsch, m.

ass, butt

Sie sagte, wenn es dir nicht passt, dann kannst du mich am Arsch lecken.

She said if you don't like it, you can kiss my ass.

Expressions including the word Arsch *are quite popular in German:*

am Arsch der Welt = *in the middle of nowhere, in a Godforsaken hole*

am/im Arsch sein = *to be screwed up*

Das geht mir am Arsch vorbei! = *I don't give a shit (about that)!*

in den Arsch gehen = *to get screwed up*

Du kannst mich (am Arsch lecken)! = *You can kiss my ass!*

Leck mich am Arsch! = *Kiss my ass!/F**k off!*

Setz deinen Arsch in Bewegung! = *Get your ass in gear!*

Arschlecker, m.

ass-kisser, brown-noser; lit. ass-licker

**Der weltweit am meisten verachtete Typ ist der soge-
nannte "Arschlecker."**
*One of the most universally disliked people in the world is the
ass-kisser.*

Arschloch, n.
a-hole, asshole
Jörg ist ein Arschloch wie er dich behandelt.
Jörg is such an asshole for treating you the way he does.

arschlos
random, pointless; lit. ass-less
Deine Idee ist total arschlos.
Your idea is completely pointless.

Mistkerl, m.
bastard, dirty swine
Du hast vielleicht Nerven hier aufzutauchen, du Mistkerl.
You've got some nerve showing up here, you bastard.

Miststück, n.
bastard, bitch; lit. piece of shit
**Dieses Miststück glaubt, sie könne mit meinem Freund
anbandeln.**
That bitch thinks she's going to make a move on my boyfriend.

*The soap "Irish Mist" made a less than spectacular
debut in Germany. It had to be renamed because Mist
means "manure" or "shit" in German. Because nobody
wanted to smell like crap, it is now called* Irisch Moos,
*"Irish Moss." Apparently smelling like a wet Irish rock is
more appealing.*

jemanden ankotzen
to be a pain in the ass
Du kotzt mich an!
You're a pain in the ass!
You puked on me!

Abtreibung, f.
abortion
Das schwangere Mädel sah keine andere Möglichkeit als die Abtreibung.
The pregnant teen felt she had no choice but to have an abortion.

abtreiben
to terminate a pregnancy, have an abortion
Obwohl meine beste Freundin erst 15 Jahre alt war, entschied sie sich nicht abzutreiben.
Even though my best friend was only 15 years old, she decided not to terminate her pregnancy.

Unaussprechlichen, pl.
unmentionables
Unsere Nachbarin hatte all ihre Unaussprechlichen an der Wäscheleine hängen.
Our neighbor had all her unmentionables hanging on the clothes line.

Unanständigkeiten, pl.
obscenities
Saras perverser Onkel erzählte ihr dreckige Witze und andere Unanständigkeiten.
Sara's perverted uncle told her dirty jokes and other obscenities.

erogene Zonen, pl.
erogenous zones
Samuel wollte alle erogenen Zonen seiner Freundin erforschen.
Samuel wanted to explore all of his girlfriend's errogenous zones.

lüstern flüstern
to whisper lustfully
Es macht mich an, wenn du lüstern in mein Ohr flüsterst.
It turns me on when you whisper lustfully in my ear.

wollüstig stöhnen
to moan ecstatically
Ich liebe es, wenn meine Freundin wollüstig stöhnt.
I love it when my girlfriend moans ecstatically.

In most of the world, male masturbation implies a dick, at least one hand, and for those who are circumsized, lubrication. While Americans grease their monkey, Germans grease their flask, den Kolben ölen. *You don't need to be a chef in order to "butter the salmon,"* den Lachs buttern—*you'll be serving up your own delicious soup,* sein eignes Süppchen kochen, *in no time. But don't forget the side dishes: German speakers also enjoy* nudelwürgen, *choking the noodle, and skinning their sausage,* sich die Wurst pellen.

Don't assume your new German friends are all clean freaks. If someone says he'd like to polish his flute, sich die Flöte polieren, *or clean his pipe,* sich die Pfeife ausklopfen, *you may be in store for a lot more.*

Wichsen, *to jerk off, can come in many forms, from the simple* Handmassage *to the Hawaii-lover's* die Palme schütteln, *to shake the palm tree. Gamblers may take the trump in the hand,* den Trumpf in die Hand nehmen *. . . a winner every time.*

For the sports enthusiast, masturbation is also known as das Taschenbillard, *pocket pool, and for those who get seasick,* einhandsegeln, *one-handed sailing, is a no-risk form of sport they can enjoy. For boxing fans, the* fünf gegen einen, *five against one, is a fight, but just who is the winner? Easy . . . it's the one left standing after ten rounds.*

Fünf gegen einen

to jerk off; lit. five against one

David war so notgeil, er beschloss, es sei Zeit für Fünf gegen einen.

David was so horny, he decided it was time to jerk off.

abmelken

to jerk off; lit. to milk

Mein Freund möchte sich ständig einen abmelken.

All my boyfriend ever wants to do is jerk off.

den Fisch fangen gehen

to masturbate; lit. to go catch the fish

Gib mir fünf Minuten im Bad, ich muss mal eben den Fisch fangen gehen.

Give me five minutes in the bathroom; I have to masturbate.

CHAPTER SIXTEEN

Die Schöne und das Biest:

S/He's Got the Look

Picture a stereotypical Swiss Miss: Is she wearing a *Dirndl* or little black dress? *Tracht*, traditional costume, is rarely seen these days, although it has retained limited popularity among the older generation in Bavaria, Switzerland, Austria, and at Munich's Oktoberfest. Regional differences abound in this area; for example, the Bavarian governor liberates his legs in *Lederhosen* for official events, while Helmut Schmidt, the former north German chancellor, proudly plays the part of sea captain in his traditional Hamburger Mütze.

Germany may not be France or Italy, but it has managed to make a name for itself in the fashion industry nonetheless. Designers including Karl Lagerfeld and Jill Sander have earned international acclaim, while supermodel Heidi Klum is one of the world's highest-earning pretty faces. Still, you may be surprised to see a segment of the German population wearing ripped acid-wash jean jackets. Yes, these Assos, "white trash," exist in *Deutschland* as well. Fortunately, if you wish to avoid them, you can hear them coming on their Harleys from miles away . . .

sich aufbretzeln

to spruce oneself up; lit. to pretzel oneself up

Ich bin gleich da, muss mich nur noch schnell aufbretzeln.

I'll be with you in a minute; I just want to spruce myself up a little.

sich aufhübschen

to pretty up

Nachdem sie sich aufgehübscht hat, sieht sie ganz passabel aus.

She looked really good after she prettied up.

sich aufmotzen

to doll oneself up

Schau mal, wie du dich heute Abend aufgemotzt hast.

Look at you; you definitely dolled yourself up tonight.

Gesichtstapete, f.

make-up; lit. face wallpaper

Guck mal, die Zicke dort hat viel zu viel Gesichtstapete.

Check out that chick with way too much make-up.

sich in Schale werfen

to be dressed to the nines; lit. to throw yourself into the peel

Dies ist ein sehr wichtiges Abendessen, da muss ich mich ordentlich in Schale werfen.

This is a very important dinner, so I'm going to be dressed to the nines.

aufporschen

to glam up; lit. to "*porsche*" up

He, wir gehen nur in die Pizzeria, warum musstest du dich denn so aufporschen?
Hey, we're only going to grab a pizza. Why did you have to glam up for that?

die Optik tunen
to get a makeover; lit. to tune the optics
Es ist an der Zeit mal deine Optik zu tunen.
I think someone is overdue for a makeover.

aufgestylt
to be trendy
Meine Schwester liebt es aufgestylt.
My sister loves to be trendy.

ausgeflippt
out of the ordinary
Für dich mag dieser rosa Pudel normal aussehen, für mich ist es ausgeflippt.
You may consider that pink poodle nothing special, but I'd call it out of the ordinary.

poppig
modern, trendy
Dein neuer Kurzhaarschnitt ist richtig poppig.
Your new short hairdo looks very modern.

niegelnagelneu
the very latest
Die gesamte Garderobe meiner Chefin ist niegelnagelneu.
My boss's entire wardrobe is the latest style.

brandneu

brand new; lit. burning new

Er hat das Geschäft mit einem brandneuen Anzug verlassen.

He left the store with a brand new suit.

der letzte Schrei

to be all the rage; lit. the latest cry

Schlaghosen scheinen wieder der letzte Schrei zu sein.

Bell bottom pants seem to be all the rage again.

der neueste Trend

the latest fad

Der neueste Trend in Musik ist Hip-hop Punk.

The latest fad in music is hip-hop punk.

ein Auslaufmodell sein

to be no spring chicken, to have numbered days; lit. discontinued model

Toms Neue ist aber auch schon ein Auslaufmodell.

Tom's new girlfriend is no spring chicken.

Tom's new girlfriend's days are numbered.

topaktuell

cutting-edge

Supermodels sind immer topaktuell was Mode anbelangt.

Supermodels are always on the cutting edge of fashion.

schnieke

well dressed, nifty, stylish

Heute siehste aber schnieke aus!

You're looking very stylish today!

ein alter Hut

old hat, out of fashion

Mir egal, ob es ein alter Hut ist, ich mag es.

I don't care if it's out of fashion; I like it.

wie aus dem Ei gepellt

spick and span; lit. peeled out of the egg

Die ganze Wohnung sah aus wie aus dem Ei gepellt, nach-dem die Putzfrau fertig war.

The entire apartment looked spick and span after the cleaning lady was finished.

Klamotten, pl.

clothes, duds

Ich denke, Klamotten machen den Mann.

I think clothes make the man.

Fummel, m.

dress; lit. rag, frock

Penelope riss sich wütend den Fummel vom Leib.

Penelope ripped off her dress furiously.

Schlüpfer, m.

undies; lit. slip-in

He Sebastian, heißer Schlüpfer, den du da heute anhast.

Hey Sebastian, those are hot undies you're wearing today.

Arsch frisst Hose

wedgie; lit. ass eats pants

Aua. Verdammt, Arsch frisst Hose . . .

Ouch. Damn, another wedgie . . .

Arschkordel, f.
G-string; lit. ass rope
Wow, schau dir mal die geile Arschkordel von der Schnitte da drüben an. Da geht mir glatt das Messer in der Hose auf!
Wow, look at the G-string on that chick over there. That gives me such a hard-on!

Arschgeweih, n.
lower back tattoo; lit. ass antlers
Ich will 'ne Frau ohne Arschgeweih.
I want a girl without a ridiculous lower back tattoo.

Schlampenstempel, m.
tramp stamp, lower back tattoo; lit. rubber stamp that reads "slut"
Angelika hat sich in Thailand einen Schlampenstempel machen lassen. Sieht total doof aus.
Angelika got a tramp stamp while she was in Thailand. It looks totally stupid.

Latschen, pl.
shoes; lit. traipse
Wirf doch endlich die alten Latschen weg.
Why don't you throw out these old shoes?

Stöckelschuhe mit Pfennigabsatz, pl.
stilettos; lit. high-heeled shoes with a penny heel
Ich frage mich, wie Frauen in Stöckelschuhen mit Pfenni-gabsatz laufen können.
It amazes me how women can walk in those stiletto heels.

Wo drückt der Schuh?, *lit. "Where does the shoe pinch?"*
means "What's the trouble?" in English. This expression
was supposedly used by Plutarch, the Greek philosopher.
He wrote that someone once demanded to know why a
certain Roman had divorced his hottie young wife. The
Roman answered that his shoe was both beautiful and
new, but he alone knew where it pinched his foot.

Zeiteisen, n.
watch; lit. time-iron
Was sagt das Zeiteisen?
What's the time?

Anatomy

Fressritze, f.
mouth; lit. munching slit
Ich hoffe, du lässt heute Abend deine Fressritze zu.
I hope you keep your mouth shut tonight.

nichts in der Birne haben
to have nothing upstairs; lit. to have nothing in the pear (which is
also a slang word for "head")
Was? Glaubst Du ich habe nichts in der Birne?
What? Do you think I have nothing upstairs?

Nuss, f.
noggin; lit. nut
Aua, ich habe mir meine Nuss angehauen.
Ouch, I banged my noggin.

(Riech)kolben, m.
schnozz; lit. (smelling) flask
Sie wäre ja sehr hübsch, wenn sie nicht so einen Kolben im Gesicht hätte.
She'd be very pretty if it weren't for that schnozz on her face.

Rettich, m.
nose; lit. radish
Mein Alter hat vielleicht einen Rettich, 'ne größere Nase hast du nicht gesehen.
My buddy has a huge nose. I bet you've never seen a bigger one.

Fresse, f.
face, bracket
Der Titel der ersten Libertine CD "Up the Bracket" übersetzt heißt "Auf die Fresse."
The title of the first Libertines CD "Up the Bracket" is called "Auf die Fresse" in German.

Wampe, f.
big belly
Zu viel Bier und zu viele Bratwürste und du bekommst eine Wampe.
Too many beers and too many sausages will give you a big belly.

Bauarbeiterdekolletee, n.
ass crack; lit. plumber's cleavage
Zieh mal deine Hose hoch. Ich seh dein Bauarbeiterdekolletee.
Pull your pants up. I can see your plumber's cleavage.

Lauscher, pl.
ears; lit. eavesdroppers

Caspar hat seine Lauscher immer für Klatsch offen.
Caspar always has his ears open for gossip.

Schnute, f.
pout; lit. snout
Zieh doch nicht so eine Schnute.
Don't pout.

die Lippen spitzen
to pucker up; lit. to sharpen the lips
Wenn du die Lippen spitzt, dann küsse ich dich.
If you pucker up, I'll kiss you.

Schnauze, f.
trap, muzzle
Halt die Schnauze!
Keep your trap shut!

Berliners are famous for their dialect. The Berliner Schnauze, lit. the Berlin muzzle, is considered to be crude by many other Germans. There is a German saying that the typical Berliner is a good-hearted big mouth.

Pornobalken, m.
ugly moustache; lit. porno balcony
Colin Farrell trägt im Film *Miami Vice* einen richtigen Pornobalken.
Colin Farrell has the ugliest moustache in the movie Miami Vice.

Schnäuzer, m.
moustache, from *schnäuzen*, to blow one's nose

Manche Frauen finden einen Mann mit Schnäuzer sexy.
Some women think a man with a moustache is sexy.

Pfote, f.
paw
Nimm deine Dreckpfoten weg von meinem iPod.
Take your dirty paws off my iPod.

Haxe, f.
knuckle
Ich glaube, ich werde heute im Restaurant eine Schweins-Haxe essen.
I think I'll eat a pig's knuckle today at the restaurant.

You don't want to tritt jemandem auf die Füße, *lit. to step on someone's feet, because it means to get on somebody's wrong side. Beware if somebody tells you that you have stepped on her big toe,* Du bist mir auf die große Zehe getreten, *since this person is telling you that you've offended her and ticked her off.*

If you want to pull someone's leg in Germany, you "take them on your arm," Jemanden auf den Arm nehmen. *This is very confusing since Germans also say* jemanden in den Arm nehmen, *meaning to hug.* Nimm mich in den Arm *means "Give me a hug."*

If a German speaker complains to you that he gives you a finger and you take his whole hand, he clearly finds you too demanding. Gib jemandem den kleinen Finger, und er nimmt die ganze Hand; *or as we might say, "Give somebody an inch, and they'll take a mile."*

Now if you've really made a German angry, she'll be ready to aus der Haut fahren, *or jump out of her skin.*

134

Physical Qualities and Defects

Muckies, pl.
muscles
Arnold Schwarzenegger ist für seine Muckies bekannt.
Arnold "the Governator" Schwarzenegger is famous for his muscles.

Karnevalsmuskeln haben
to be a weakling; lit. to have carnival muscles
Na komm schon, drück die Hantel richtig hoch. Oder hast du etwa nur Karnevalsmuskeln?
Come on, lift that dumbbell! Or are you a weakling?

Rettungsring, m.
love handles, spare tire; lit. life preserver
Steffi liebt alles an Matthias, sogar seinen Rettungsring.
Steffi loves everything about Matthias, including his spare tire.

üppig
voluptuous, busty; lit. abundant
Die meisten Männer mögen üppige Frauen.
Most men love busty women.

eine kesse Eva
saucy (little) thing
Sie ist eine kesse Eva.
She's a saucy little thing.

auf Draht sein
to be in good form
Beim heutigen Tennismatch hoffe ich auf Draht zu sein.
I hope to be in good form for today's tennis match.

Dampfwalze, f.
fatso; lit. steamroller
Achtung, die Dampfwalze kommt. Geht aus dem Weg, sonst gibt es Verletzte!
Watch out, fatso's coming. Get out of the way or you'll get hurt!

Pommespanzer, m.
fattie; lit. French fries tank
Einige Fluggesellschaften wollen Pommespanzer zwei Sitzplätze berechnen.
Some airlines want to charge fatties for two seats.

hausbacken
homely, dowdy; lit. home-baked
Warum werden eigentlich immer nur Frauen und nicht Männer als hausbacken bezeichnet?
Why is it that it's always women who are called homely and never men?

Mauerblümchen, n.
wallflower
In der Schule trug ich dicke Brillengläser und wurde nie zum Tanzen aufgefordert—ich war ein Mauerblümchen
In high school I wore thick glasses and was never asked to any dance—a real wallflower.

hässlich wie die Nacht sein
to be hit with the ugly stick; lit. to be ugly like the night
Deine Freundin ist hässlich wie die Nacht.
Your girlfriend looks like she's been hit with the ugly stick.

Augenweide, f.
easy on the eyes

Heidi Klum ist eine wahre Augenweide.
Heidi Klum is easy on the eyes.

Plagegeist, n.
nuisance; lit. plague ghost
Dein kleiner Bruder ist ein Plagegeist.
Your little brother is a nuisance.

Platzhirsch, m.
top dog; lit. top deer
Heinz macht in seiner Firma eine steile Karriere. Bald wird er der Platzhirsch sein.
Heinz is making a good career for himself in his company. Soon he may be the top dog.

Platzhirschverhalten, n.
top dog behavior
Platzhirschverhalten kann zu großer Arroganz führen.
Top dog behavior can often lead to arrogance.

Klette, f.
obsessed girlfriend; lit. clinger
Es war zwar schwer, aber endlich wurde er die Klette los.
It was hard, but he finally broke up with his obsessed girlfriend.

Klammeraffe, m.
obsessed guy; lit. clinging monkey
Martha konnte es nicht fassen, als der Klammeraffe von einem Freund per SMS-Nachricht mit ihr Schluss machte.
Martha couldn't believe it when her obsessed boyfriend broke up with her by text message.

Tantenverführer, m.

young man with suspiciously good manners; lit. aunt-seducer

Daniel war so ein Tantenverführer, wir dachten, da stimmt was nicht.

Daniel had such suspiciously good manners, we thought something wasn't quite right.

Braut, f.

chick; lit. bride

He, schau dir mal die Braut dort an!

Hey, check out that chick!

steiler Zahn, m.

fox, lit. steep tooth

Beyonce ist ein steiler Zahn; sie hat Beine bis zum Hals und scharfe Kurven.

Beyonce is a fox; she has legs that go on forever and great curves.

blondes Gift, n.

blond bombshell; lit. blond poison

Warte, bis du meine Kusine kennenlernst—die ist blondes Gift.

Wait until you meet my cousin—she's a blond bombshell.

Muskelprotz, m.

buff guy, beefcake

Vielen Frauen können Muskelprotzen nicht viel abgewinnen.

Many women don't see the attraction of a buff guy.

Zahnstocher, m.

skinny, weak guy, wimp; lit. toothpick

Nimm mal einer den Zahnstocher aus dem Weg!

Somebody get rid of this skinny guy!

CHAPTER 17

Die Schöne und das Biest II:

Looks Aren't Everything

They say that if heaven is a hotel where the food is French, the service is English, the entertainment is Italian, and the security is German, then hell is a hotel where the food is English, the service is French, the entertainment is German, and the security is Italian. If entertainment tastes are a window into a culture, what does that say about the German personality?

Stereotypes abound, both positive and negative, but Germans are often seen as order-obsessed, eager, nature-loving, and beer-guzzling all at once. However, there are two sides to every coin: the obsession with order in Germany (and other German-speaking countries) may be stifling at times, but you'll take trains that run on time and find the city streets clean. Being forced to recycle your trash and separate paper from plastic may be added work, but you'll reap the benefits in the form of lovely nature preserves, public parks, and clean water.

Charakterzüge—Character Traits

die Nase hoch tragen
to have one's nose in the air, to be arrogant; lit. to carry the nose high
Du kannst deine Nase nicht höher tragen als er.
You can't be more arrogant than he is.

spießig
square, narrow-minded
Du bist so spießig, aber Schatz, was macht das schon.
You're so square, but baby, I don't care.

Petze, f.
tattletale
Niemand kann eine Petze leiden.
Nobody likes a tattletale.

Quasselstrippe, f.
chatterbox
Eine Quasselstrippe ist jederzeit bereit ihre Meinung zu allen und allem zu geben.
A chatterbox is always ready to give her opinion to anyone on any and every subject.

Warmduscher, m.
wimp; lit. warm-showerer
Ich möchte nicht mit so einem Warmduscher wie dir zusammen gesehen werden.
I don't want to be seen with a wimp like you.

Tugendbold, m.
goody-goody
Sie hatte das Gefühl, dass er ein zu großer Tugendbold war.
She felt he was just too much of a goody-goody.

Pantoffelheld, m.
henpecked husband; lit. bedroom slipper hero
Meine Tante genoss es einen Pantoffelhelden zu haben, dem sie Befehle erteilen konnte.
My aunt loved having a henpecked husband she could order around.

Schlappschwanz, m.
wuss; lit. limp dick
Dein Bruder ist ja ein Schlappschwanz. Er traut sich nicht mal aufs Motorrad.
Your brother is a wuss. He doesn't even dare ride a motorcycle.

Jammerlappen, m.
sissy
Frieder ist so ein Jammperlappen, anstatt mit uns in der Stadt Schnecken checken zu gehen, bleibt er zu Hause.
Frieder is such a sissy, instead of coming with us to check out girls downtown, he is staying home.

Schürzenjäger, m.
skirt chaser; lit. apron hunter
Meine beste Freundin hat einen Schürzenjäger geheiratet.
My best friend married a skirt chaser.

schweigen wie ein Grab
to keep a secret; lit. to be quiet as a grave
Du kannst meinem Mann ruhig alles anvertrauen, der plappert nichts aus. Er kann schweigen wie ein Grab.
You can tell my husband anything, he won't give it away. He can keep a secret.

sich querstellen
to put a stop to something, put one's foot down; lit. to block

Veronique konnte nicht begreifen, warum ausgerechnet Dylan sich immer querstellen musste.
Veronique couldn't understand why it was always Dylan who insisted on putting his foot down.

Memme, f.
sissy
Mit Klaus für den Marathonlauf zu trainieren war eine blöde Idee. Er ist 'ne Memme.
It was a terrible idea to train for the marathon with Klaus. He's a sissy.

Hasenfuß, m.
coward; lit. rabbit's foot
Für einen Hasenfuß ist es schwer Respekt zu gewinnen.
It's hard for a coward to gain respect.

Heulsuse, f.
cry baby; lit. crying Susie
Barbaras kleiner Bruder ist so eine Heulsuse.
Barbara's little brother is such a cry baby.

Rüpel, m.
rogue, lout
Der Latin Lover, der Anna geschwängert hatte, war offenbar auch noch ein ziemlicher Rüpel.
Apparently, the Latin lover who knocked Anna up was also a real lout.

Trottel, m.
klutz; also jerk, idiot
Ich habe einen ganzen Teller Suppe verschüttet, was bin ich für einen Trottel.
I spilled an entire bowl of soup; I'm such a klutz.

Einfaltspinsel, m.

simpleton; lit. oafish brush

Nach zwei Wochen hatte Bettina bemerkt, dass ihr Schwarm zwar Muskeln hatte, aber sonst ein Einfaltspinsel war.

After two weeks, Bettina realized that while her crush did have nice muscles, he was a real simpleton.

Aufschneider, m.

braggart, boaster

Wenn sie nicht so ein Aufschneider wäre, fände ich sie ganz attraktiv.

If she wasn't such a boaster, I would find her attractive.

Arschkriecher, m.

brown-noser, suck-up; lit. ass crawler, as in crawling up someone's ass

Nach dem Seminar wartete eine Reihe von Arschkriechern auf den Professor.

After class, there was a line of brown-nosers waiting for the professor.

Großkotz, m.

showoff

Sei mal nicht so ein Großkotz. Das glaubt dir doch kein Mensch!

Don't be such a showoff. Nobody will buy that story!

Spargeltarzan, m.

weakling; lit. asparagus tarzan

Der Spargeltarzan sollte schleunigst mal ins Fitness-Studio gehen.

This weakling should get himself to the gym right away.

Schaumschläger, m.

braggart; lit. foam thrower

Tom gibt mit seinem Können an, aber wir wissen, dass er nur ein Schaumschläger ist.

Tom speaks of his amazing abilities, but we know he's only a braggart.

Badewannenpisser, m.

childish person; lit. bathwater pisser

Mit so einem Badewannenpisser wie du möchte ich mich nicht abgeben.

I don't want to waste my time with someone as childish as you.

sich benehmen wie eine offene Hose

to misbehave; lit. to behave like a pair of unzipped pants

Das darf ja wohl nicht wahr sein! Der kommt hier ungeladen rein und benimmt sich wie 'ne offene Hose.

I don't believe it! He shows up here uninvited and behaves like a jerk.

Kratzbürste, f.

shrew; lit. scratching brush

Kannst du die Kratzbürste bändigen?

Can you tame the shrew?

knorke

cool, great

Danke, dass du das für mich gemacht hast, du bist echt knorke!

Thanks for doing that for me, you are way cool!

lasch

uncool

Der Abend war total lasch. Ich glaube, Zähne ziehen macht mehr Spaß.

This evening was so uncool. I think I would have had more fun getting a tooth pulled.

Fußabtreter, m.

doormat

Ich hab's satt! Ich hab keinen Bock hier als Fußabtreter herzuhalten!

I'm tired of being everybody's doormat around here!

Maschine, f.

da man; lit. machine

Der Johann hat heute dreißig Bäume gefällt, ist voll die Maschine.

Johann cut down thirty trees today. He's da man.

halbes Hemd

puny runt; lit. half a shirt

Du kannst nicht mal meinen Koffer heben! Du bist ja ein ganz schön halbes Hemd!

You can't even lift my suitcase! What a puny runt!

geiler Bock, m.

horny old goat

Die junge Frau war den Annäherungsversuchen des geilen Bocks erlegen.

The young lady succumbed to the advances of the horny old rich guy.

CHAPTER 18

Du meine Seele, du mein Herz:

Love Is a Wonderful Thing

From the majestic Alps to the topless beaches of the North Sea, Germany offers the perfect setting for falling in love. You may not find refined French sweet talk or hot-headed Mediterranean passion here, but the Germans can and do enthrall with their moody brand of Romanticism. Called *Sturm und Drang*, storm and passion, it encompasses both the highest of highs and the lowest of lows. Love is equal parts elation and sorrow, these drama queens believe, and to feel something is better than to feel nothing at all.

That said, German Romanticism embraced these ideals in order to distance itself from French Classicism, which preferred sedate, rational thinking. So it turns out that when it comes to love, those strict, order-obsessed Germans aren't so uptight after all. Still, some habits die hard, and you'll find some of the ways love is described in German to be oddly mechanical: True love never dies is expressed as *Alte Liebe rostet nicht*, lit. "old love doesn't rust."

solo sein
to be single
Die meisten jungen Männer genießen es, solo zu sein.
Most young guys enjoy being single.

mit jemanden gehen
to date someone; lit. to go with someone
Henriette wollte mit jemandem gehen, bei dem sie keine Chancen hatte.
Henriette wanted to date someone she didn't have a chance with.

verknallt
in love, infatuated
Sie waren frisch verknallt.
They had just fallen in love.

in jemanden verknallt sein
to have a crush on somebody
Martin ist total verknallt in Silke.
Martin has a huge crush on Silke.

verschossen (in jemanden) sein
to be infatuated or crazy about someone; lit. to be shot into
Er ist total verschossen in sie.
He's totally nuts about her.

Schmetterlinge im Bauch haben
to have butterflies in one's stomach
Der Torwart erklärte, er habe vor jedem Spiel Schmetterlinge im Bauch.
The goalkeeper said he always had butterflies in his stomach before a game.

Liebespaar, n.
couple, item; lit. love pair
Angela und Kurt sind seit zwei Monaten ein Liebespaar.
Angela und Kurt have been an item for two months now.

wahre Liebe, f.
true love, love of one's life
Die wahre Liebe trifft man—wenn überhaupt—nur einmal im Leben.
You only meet the love of your life once, if at all.

Liebesgeschichte, f.
love story
Ihre Liebesgeschichte begann in der Schlange an der Supermarktkasse.
Their love story began in the supermarket checkout line.

auf jemanden stehen
to have the hots for someone; lit. to stand on someone
Igitt, sag bloß nicht, du stehst auf den eingebildeten Lackaffen dort drüben!
Arrrgh, don't tell me you've got the hots for that conceited jerk over there!

jemanden anhimmeln
to make goo-goo eyes at someone; lit. to look up enraptured at someone
Das Letzte, was ich brauche ist, dass meine Schwester ihn anhimmelt.
The last thing I need is my sister making goo-goo eyes at him.

jemanden vergöttern
to adore someone

Du weißt nicht, wie es ist jemanden zu vergöttern.
You don't know what it's like to adore someone.

Schwarm, m.
crush, heartthrob
Richard ist seit Schulzeiten Nancy Schwarm.
Richard has been Nancy's heartthrob since high school.

abgöttisch lieben
to be madly in love
Die Studentin ist nur fünfzehn Jahre alt und glaubt ihren Lehrer abgöttisch zu lieben.
The student is only fifteen years old and thinks she's madly in love with her teacher.

vergeben sein
to be already taken
Tut mir leid, dass ich nicht mit dir tanzen kann, aber ich bin schon vergeben.
I'm sorry I can't dance with you, but I'm already taken.

noch zu haben sein
to be available
Ich bin schon vergeben, aber meine Kusine ist noch zu haben.
I'm already taken, but my cousin is still available.

Schleimer, m.
slimeball
Heidi ist so peinlich; warum geht sie mit so einem alten Schleimer wie er?
Heidi is so pathetic. Why does she go out with a slimeball like him?

Süßholz raspeln

to sweet–talk; lit. to grate *Süßholz*, a root used to make licorice-flavored syrup

Er ist vielleicht nicht der Beste im Bett, aber mein Ex konnte bei jeder Frau gut Süßholz raspeln.

He may not be the best in bed, but my ex-boyfriend sure knew how to sweet talk a lady.

zum Anbeißen (gut) aussehen

to look good enough to eat

Boah, als sie im Klub erschien, sah sie zum Anbeißen gut aus.

Wow, she showed up at the club looking good enough to eat.

treulose Tomate, f.

fair-weather friend; lit. disloyal tomato

Eines Tages wirst du selbst merken, dass Hannah nur eine treulose Tomate ist.

You'll find out someday that Hannah's just a fair-weather friend.

im siebten Himmel sein

to be on cloud nine; lit. to be in seventh heaven

Nach seiner Verabredung mit Sabine war Rupert im siebten Himmel.

After his date with Sabine, Rupert was on cloud nine.

das gewisse Etwas haben

to have a certain something

Ich kann es nicht genau erklären warum ich Gerhardt mag . . . er hat einfach das gewisse Etwas.

I don't know why I like Gerhardt . . . he just has a certain something.

baggern

to flirt; lit. to dig

Rita hat auf der Party gebaggert wie ein Weltmeister.

Rita flirted like a pro at the party.

jemanden reizen

to attract someone

Du musst schnell handeln und einen kühlen Kopf bewahren, wenn du jemanden reizen möchtest.

You better act fast and think straight if you want to attract someone.

Aufreißer, m.

player

Kathrin dachte, sie hätte in Tim ihre wahre Liebe gefunden, aber sie fand bald heraus, daß er nur ein alter Aufreißer war.

Kathrin thought she had found the love of her life when she met Tim, but she soon realized that he was nothing but a player.

Anmache, f.

come on

Ich habe ihre freundlichen Worte gehört und warte jetzt auf die Anmache.

I listened to all her friendly talk and now I'm waiting for the come on.

jemanden anmachen

to hit on someone

Ich komme total müde von der Arbeit mit dem Bus heim und der Depp denkt, er müsse mich anmachen.

I was coming home from work on the bus, competely exhausted, and that dumb guy thought he needed to hit on me.

etwas miteinander anfangen

to get it on with someone

Erinnerst du dich, was Marvin Gaye in seinem Lied sagt: "Let's get it on"—lass uns was miteinander anfangen.

Remember what Marvin Gaye said: "Let's get it on."

sich Hals über Kopf in jemanden zu verlieben

to fall head over heels in love with someone

Das Letzte, mit dem ich gerechnet habe, war mich Hals über Kopf in die Schwester meines besten Freundes zu verlieben.

The last thing I ever expected was to fall head over heels in love with my best friend's sister.

jemanden zum Fressen gern haben

to love someone to bits

Jennifer hat ihren Mann zum Fressen gern.

Jennifer loves her husband to bits.

jemandem den Partner ausspannen

to steal someone's partner; lit. to unhitch or pinch someone's partner

Das Schlimmste, was du einem Freund antun kannst, ist seinen Partner auszuspannen.

The worst thing you can do to a friend is to steal their partner.

züngeln

to French kiss; lit. to tongue

Dieser Knilch wollte schon eine Stunde, nachdem ich ihn kennengelernt hatte, mit mir züngeln.

This guy wanted to French kiss an hour after I first met him.

fremdgehen

to cheat on one's partner; lit. to go strange or external

Wenn du ans Fremdgehen denkst, dann rechne damit erwischt zu werden.

If you're going to cheat on your partner, expect to get caught.

Seitensprung, m.

infidelity, to have a bit on the side; lit. jump to the side

Viele verheiratete Paare halten einen Seitensprung nicht für ausgeschlossen.

Many married couples keep open the possibility to have a bit on the side.

Techtelmechtel, n.

love affair

Caroline hat ein Techtelmechtel mit dem Freund ihres Mackers.

Caroline is having an affair with her boyfriend's best friend.

Liebeskummer, m.

lovesick

Hab keinen Liebeskummer wegen dem Arschloch!

Don't be so lovesick over that jerk!

Katzenjammer, m.

heartache; lit. cat's wailing

Manchmal führt eine Romanze zu Katzenjammer hinterher.

Sometimes romance can lead to heartache.

Knutschfleck, m.

hickey

Ist das ein Knutschfleck an deinem Hals?

Is that a hickey on your neck?

füßeln

to play footsie

Während des Essens haben sie gefüßelt.
During the dinner they played footsie.

verführen
to seduce
Viele Kerle wollen Frauen nur verführen und lassen sie hinterher links liegen.
Plenty of guys only want to seduce women and then discard them.

sich verabreden
to make a date
Es gibt in der Kneipe freitags eine tolle "Happy Hour," lass uns dort verabreden.
There's a great Happy Hour special on Fridays at the bar, so let's make a date.

kuscheln
to cuddle, to snuggle up
Wir haben uns irgendwo ein abgelegenes Plätzchen zum Kuscheln gesucht.
We looked for a secluded spot to snuggle up.

sich umarmen
to embrace, to hold, to hug
Es gibt nichts Schöneres als meine Freundin zu umarmen.
There's nothing better than holding my girlfriend.

Abfuhr, f.
rebuff, rejection
James hat seine Kollegin gefragt, ob sie mit ihm gehen will und bekam eine Abfuhr.
James asked his colleague out and was rejected.

sich eine Abfuhr holen

to be snubbed

Elke rechnete damit, fürs Team gewählt zu werden, aber sie hat sich später eine Abfuhr geholt.

Elke thought she would be selected for the team but she found out later she had been snubbed.

einen Korb bekommen

to be rejected; lit. to receive a basket

In einer Beziehung tut es immer besonders weh, wenn man einen Korb bekommt.

In dating, it always hurts if you're the one who gets rejected.

gehörnter Eheman, m.

cuckold; lit. horned husband

Es wurden schon viele Geschichten über den gehörnten Ehemann geschrieben.

There have been many stories written about the cuckold husband.

kletten

to smother

Ich muss mit ihr Schluss machen, sie klettet zu sehr.

I have to break up with Natalie; she's smothering me.

wie eine Klette

like a limpet, like glue

So sehr ich auch versuche ihn loszuwerden, er klebt noch immer wie eine Klette an mir.

As much as I try to get rid of him, he sticks to me like glue.

jemandem den Laufpass geben

to dump someone; lit. to give someone walking papers

Mickey war total schockiert, als Gwen ihm den Laufpass gab.
Mickey was totally shocked when Gwen dumped him.

jemanden abservieren
to ditch somebody; lit. to clear the table
Nach unserer gemeinsamen Nacht hat sie mich ganz kalt abserviert.
After the night we spent together, she coldly ditched me.

Schluss machen
break up
Der beste Teil am miteinander Schluss machen ist, wenn man sich wieder verträgt.
The best part of a break up is when you make up again.

die Kurve kriegen
make the leap; lit. to make the curve
Nach zehnjähriger Ehe war ihnen klar, sie konnten die Kurve nicht kriegen und so trennten sie sich.
After ten years, the couple decided they couldn't make the leap so, they separated.

CHAPTER 19

Drang nach Sex:

Partners and Their Private Parts

Perhaps you're learning Dirty German to help with your studies, or simply for your own pleasure. In either case, traveling to the German-speaking world is not a complete journey without physical experiences to harden your memories. For some, this state can be reached after a fine sausage and a beer; for others, this involves a different kind of meat. In order to wholly immerse yourself, you must allow German culture to penetrate you deeply. When it comes to sex, Germans may not have invented the wheel, but the proud creators of Mercedes Benz will be happy to take you for a ride.

But in a country with 80 million citizens, you've got to find the right German for your needs (this is best done before that third beer). Whether you're in search of a gorgeous goody-goody or a lascivious ladies man, your chances of scoring are greatly improved with the following vocabulary. And we all know that finding the right partner is not just a question of personality . . . there is also the small, or large, matter of their private parts. If you're still looking for your true love in vain, why not lower your standards and settle for just a piece of it?

notgeil
horny

Der Typ ist echt notgeil. Wenn der an was anderes als Sex denken würde, wäre ich echt überrascht.

That guy is really horny. If he thinks about anything other than sex, I'd be surprised.

brünstig
in heat

Schau mal, wie sich die Inge an jeden Typen schmeißt. Ich glaube, die ist brünstig.

Do you see how Inge throws herself at every guy? I think she's in heat.

heiß sein
to be hot

Alter, ich habe die Irene gestern noch mitgenommen. Die war doch heiß wie Frittierfett!

Homey, I took Irene home with me last night. She was as hot as frying oil!

dicke Eier haben
to be damn horny; lit. to have big eggs (nuts)

Boah, Alter, ich hab verdammt dicke Eier, ich muss ficken!

Dude, I'm so damn horny, I need to f**k now!

Kavaliersschmerzen, pl.
blue balls; lit. gentleman's pain

Ihre Zurückhaltung war die Ursache für meine Kavaliersschmerzen.

Her reluctance led to my blue balls.

fickbar
f**kable
Er ist nicht der Tollste, aber fickbar.
He's not great, but he's f**kable.

geiles Karnickel, n.
horndog
Micha hat sich schon wieder im Bad einen abgewichst. Was für'n geiles Karnickel.
Micha was jerking off in the men's bathroom again. What a horndog, eh?

geiler Hund, m.
horndog
Nenn mich einen geilen Hund!
Just call me a horndog!

Weiberheld, m.
lady-killer
Mein Opa war zu seiner Zeit ein richtiger Weiberheld.
In his time, my grandpa was a real lady-killer.

Penispirat, m.
womanizer; lit. penis pirate
Mann, der Ben hat gestern Abend schon wieder eine weggefickt; der is mal 'n richtiger Penispirat!
Damn, Ben was f**king another girl last night; he's the biggest womanizer!

Hurenbock, m.
male slut; lit. whore buck

Kurt: "Oh Mann, ich muss heute Abend dringend noch was aufreißen. " Peter: "Alter Hurenbock."
Kurt: "Ohhhh, I need to get laid tonight." Peter: "You are nothing but a slut."

Flittchen, n.
hussy
Ich möchte wissen, was Clemens an dem Flittchen findet.
I'd like to know what Clemens sees in that hussy.

Schickse, f.
slut
Deine Freundin is 'ne olle Schickse.
Your girlfriend is a slut.

Schlampe, f.
tramp
Jasmin, so angezogen gehst du mir nicht aus dem Haus. Du siehst aus wie eine Schlampe.
Jasmin, you're not leaving the house dressed like that. You look like a tramp.

Heißmacherin, f.
tease; lit. one who heats (someone else)
Die Thea ist 'ne Heißmacherin. Sie sollte einen endlich ranlassen.
Thea is such a tease. She should just put out already.

aufheizen
to tease
Hör auf, mich aufzuheizen.
Stop teasing me.

nichts anbrennen lassen

to be on the make; lit. to not let anything scorch

Er lässt nichts anbrennen. Tina sollte sein nächstes Opfer werden.

He is always on the make. Tina is supposed to be his next victim.

gut im Bett sein

to be good in bed

Ich wette, dass Jörg gut im Bett ist.

I bet Jörg would be good in bed.

Schwanzfopper, m.

cock-tease

Du weißt was Nadia für ein Schwanzfopper ist.

You know what a cock-tease Nadia is.

Schwanzmagnet, m.

hot mama; lit. dick magnet

Schau dir mal diesen Schwanzmagnet an der Theke an.

Would you look at the hot mama at the bar?

Anstandsfick, m.

courtesy f**k

Mein Date gestern war beschissen, ich hab sie den ganzen Abend durchgefüttert und sie hat nicht mal 'nen Anstands- fick angeboten.

My date yesterday sucked. I wined and dined her all night long and she didn't even offer a courtesy f**k.

Minorities

bi

bisexual

Ich glaube, die Petra is bi.
I think Petra is bi.

schwul
gay
Der Dieter ist ja schwuler als 'ne Handtasche voller Regenbogen!
Dieter is gayer than a handbag full of rainbows!

warmer Bruder, m.
gay, homosexual; lit. warm brother
Ich bin mir sicher, der Danni will nichts von deiner Freundin, der ist ein warmer Bruder!
I'm sure Danni doesn't want anything from your girlfriend, he's gay.

Analritter, m.
fag; lit. anal knight
Ja, mein Vater das ist ein Analritter! Hast Du ein Problem damit?
Yes, my dad's a faggot! You got a problem with that?

für die andere Mannschaft spielen
to play for the other team
Der Giovanni ist knackig, aber er spielt leider für die andere Mannschaft.
Giovanni is sexy, but unfortunately he plays for the other team.

Lesbe, f.
lesbian
Die Lesbe war entsetzt über die Ignoranz ihres Nachbarn.
The lesbian was shocked how narrow-minded her neighbor was.

Germay boasts plenty of homosexuals, but Cologne and Berlin are the two cities with the largest and most active gay communities. The Schwules Museum in Berlin is also the largest gay museum in Europe, and features rotating exhibitions as well as an extensive library and archives.

kesser Vater, m.
dyke, butch lesbian; lit. cheeky father
Meine Cousine ist ein kesser Vater.
My cousin is a dyke.

Leckschwester, f.
lesbo; lit. lick-sister
Silvie ist'ne kleine Leckschwester, wenn du mich fragst.
Silvie is a little lesbo, if you ask me.

Schokostecher, m.
fudgepacker; lit. chocolate stabber
Der Steven treibt's nur mit Männern. Das ist voll der Schokostecher.
Steven only f**ks guys. He's a complete fudgepacker.

175er, m.
homo
Kalle: "Schau' dir 'mal die Lederuschi an. "Uwe: "Wen?" Kalle: "Den 175er."
Kalle: "Look at that guy in leather." Uwe: "Who?" Kalle: "The homo."

If you are a history buff, you may refer to gay person as a 175er. The term dates back to 1872 and refers to § 175 of the StGB (the German book of law), which forbade homosexuality. This clause was finally abolished in the 1990s after the reunification of Germany, but the slang term is used to this day.

Tunte, f.
tranny, fairy, queen
In diesem Club laufen ganz schön viele Tunten rum.
There are an awful lot of trannies in this nightclub.

Schwanzlutscher, m.
cock-sucker
Meine ex-Freundin war ein guter Schwanzlutscher.
My ex-girlfriend was a good cock-sucker.

a tergo
doggy style
Ich will's heut a tergo.
Today I wanna do it doggy style.

flachlegen
to screw somebody
Haste die Mandy gestern eigentlich noch flach gelegt oder hat sie sich geziert?
Did you manage to screw Mandy last night or did she have 'morals'?

Sex Parts

Möpse, pl.
tits, boobs
Das sind vielleicht pralle Möpse.
That's some set of tits.

Vorbau m.
rack; lit. porch
Geiler Vorbau!
Nice rack!

ganz schön Holz vor der Hütte
knockers; lit. plenty of wood in front of the hut
Du hast ganz schön ordentlich Holz vor der Hütte!
What a nice pair of knockers you have!

kein Holz vor der Hütte
flat-chested; lit. no wood in front of the hut
Manche Männer mögen Frauen ohne viel Holz vor der Hütte.
Some guys like their women flat-chested.

Kisten, pl.
tits; lit. box, chest
Andere Männer mögen Frauen mit großen Kisten.
Other guys like their women with big tits.

(Scham)lippen, pl.
pussy lips
Frauen haben vier Lippen. Zwei zum Scheiße labern und zwei um es wiedergutzumachen.
Women have four lips. Two for talking shit and two to make up for it.

Latte, f.
hard-on; lit. lath
Deine Latte hebt den Tisch hoch.
Your hard-on is lifting the table.

Jungfernhäutchen, n.
cherry, hymen; lit. maidenhead
Ich möchte nur Sex ohne Jungfernhäutchen.
I only want sex when I don't have to pop a cherry.

Po, m.
butt
Gefällt dir mein Po?
Do you like my butt?

After, m.
anus, rectum
Der Arzt musste seinen After checken.
The doctor had to check his rectum.

analfixiert
anal retentive
Mein Vater ist so analfixiert.
My father is so anal retentive.

Schoßglatze, f.
circumcised; lit. the bald-headed lap
Die meisten Amerikaner haben 'ne Schoßglatze, die meisten Deutschen keine.
Most American men are circumcised, while most Germans aren't.

Aal, m.
shlong; lit. eel
Mach mal deinen Stall zu, sonst fällt noch dein Aal raus.
Zip up or your shlong will fall out.

Fleischpeitsche, f.

dick; lit. meat whip (used in the movie *Juno*)

Den Tom willst du nicht kennenlernen, sag ich dir. Der hat 'ne richtige Fleischpeitsche—sehr böses Kaliber!

You really don't want to meet Tom, I tell you. He's got a some mean cock!

Lit. You really don't want to meet Tom, I tell you. He's got a real meat whip—very mean caliber!

Pimmel, m.

penis

Mein Pimmel ist mein bester Freund.

My penis is my best friend.

Salami mit Puls, f.

meat popsicle; lit. salami with a pulse

Du willst Salami? Ich geb' dir Salami mit Puls.

You want a popsicle? I can give you a meat popsicle.

Spermalanze, f.

dick; lit. sperm lance

Warte nur, bis meine Spermalanze dich trifft.

Just wait until you get hit with my dick.

Hodensack, m.

scrotum

Arianna spielt gerne an seinem Hodensack rum.

Arianna loves to play around with his scrotum.

Sack, m.

(nut)sack

Dann hat sie sanft seinen Sack gedrückt.

Then she gently squeezed his nutsack.

Schwanz, m.
dick; lit. tail
Kein Schwanz ist so hart wie das Leben!
No dick is as hard as life!

Stopfer, m.
dick; lit. plunger
Sein Stopfer kam zum Einsatz.
His dick was on a mission.

Kronjuwelen, pl.
crown jewels, family jewels
Vorsicht mit den Kronjuwelen!
Don't hurt the family jewels!

Marriages end in divorce for many reasons, but sex and money problems top the list in German-speaking countries. It doesn't matter if you're a woman or a man, dick will always end up as das Alimentenkabel, *the alimony cable. Before you say "I do," be sure it's not too short . . .*

Strength and the search for power is associated with both dicks and Germans alike. The tiny limp penis becomes ein Geschlechtsriese, *a sex giant, or* der Hauptgenerator, *the main generator. Warriors will compare it to* ein Beckenbrecher, *a pelvis breaker,* eine Liebeslanze, *a love lance, and* eine Spermaschleuder, *a cum slingshot. Royalty buffs will honor* der Zepter der Liebe, *the scepter of love, and the precious* Kronjuwelen, *crown jewels (testicles). Custom dictates that you should kneel down in order to greet his majesty! From more simple origins,* der Rüssel, *the (tree) trunk, conveys length, width, and hardness, and is certain to please every nature-lover.*

For those with a sweet tooth, Germans will offer you a meat candy, Bonbon aus Wurst, *or some* Liebeslolli, *love lollipops. One may take you out to have* eine Bockwurst mit Pulsschlag, *a sausage with a pulse, or* eine Supernudel, *a super noodle. The two fields in which German culture excels, cold cuts and music, to promote another area they are just as fond of, but slightly less good at: sex.* Die Fleischflöte, *the meat flute, will not only entrance a partner, but feed them too. In case of a sex emergency,* der Feuerwehrmann, *the firefighter, will come to put out the fire that is burning inside you.*

Germany is the country of unlimited speeding, powerful autos, and the ancestors of modern rockets. Take der Rosa Porsche, *the pink Porsche, for a ride. For those who ask for the moon, we recommend the* die rote Rakete, *the red rocket, instead.*

If you play the beauty, Germans will provide the beast. Die einäugige Hosenschlange, *the one-eyed trouser snake, clearly sees your darker side and* der Hosenwurm, *the trouser worm, will be pleased to dig even deeper. Speaking of holes,* der Spaltentaucher, *the crevice-diver, is the one to call if you're feeling empty. Finally, if you feel uncomfortable about these expressions and are just looking for an average German Joe, ask for it as simple as it comes:* Johannes, *Johnny.*

Scheide, f.

vagina

Sybille hat ihre Scheide beim Gynäkologen untersucht bekommen.

Sybille had her vagina examined at the gynecologist.

Kitzler, m.

clit

Lass mich dir einen Tipp geben: Frauen mögen es, wenn man sie am Kitzler kitzelt.

Let me give you some advice: women like it when you play with their clits.

Puderdose, f.

box, vagina; lit. powder compact

Lass mich mit deiner Puderdose pudern.

Let me bang your box.

Lit. Let me powder with your powder compact.

Muschi, f.

pussy

Ich weiß nie, ob du von Muschi der Katze oder von der anderen Muschi sprichst . . .

I never know whether you are talking about the 'pussy' cat or the other pussy . . .

Möse, f.

pussy

Die Britta steht total auf Möse lecken.

Britta loves to have her pussy licked.

Sex is a favorite sport in Germany and like any other game, there are both offensive and defensive tactics. If men stand behind their weapons, women had better head for cover in their Schützengraben, *trench. Do-it-yourselfers may compare their dicks to drills, which makes the corresponding pussy a* Bohrloch, *drill hole. Its appearance itself gave birth to* die Fotze, *gash, die*

Fleischfalte, meat crease, der Schlitz, groove, and die Lustfurche, groove of desire.

The main inspiration, however, is still the vagina's lumen or hollowness. Surprising associations are made with this empty organ. If you're thirsty, you may consider looking for eine Dose, *a can, of your favorite beverage. First, don't forget to check the expiration date before you pop it. Next, don't shake it too much or it will squirt in your face. If you're looking for adventure or a hook-up, be sure to visit to the tasty* Lachshöhle, *lit. salmon cave. If treasure hunting is your passion or Indiana Jones your hero, there's no need to travel around the world. Any woman nearby has a* Jadekästchen, *jade box, that is waiting to be discovered.*

Even if German men take good care of their bodies, they aren't ready for make-up yet. That said, even the most masculine German will ask to use his girlfriend's Puderdose, *powder compact, once in a while.*

Car lovers in need of a service can head to the Pimmelgarage, *penis garage. Just avoid bringing in your hearse, unless of course you're willing to offer Johnny* eine Schwanzschatulle, *a dick casket.*

Tools

Gummi, m.
rubber, condom
Ohne Gummi läuft nichts.
No rubber, no sex.

Präser, m.
condom

Hast du'n Präser dabei?
Did you bring a condom?

Vibrator, m.
vibrator
Ich habe mir den Vibrator aus der Serie "Sex and the City" gekauft.
I bought the vibrator they talked about on "Sex and the City."

Mösenmoped, n.
vibrator; lit. vagina moped
Ich mag's, wenn meine Freudin vor meinen Augen mit ihrem Mösenmoped rumspielt.
I like it when my girlfriend plays around with her vibrator in front of me.

Dildo, n.
dildo
Beim Suchen nach der Katze hat Chris das Dildo seiner Mutter unterm Bett gefunden.
While looking for the cat, Chris found his mom's dildo under the bed.

CHAPTER 20

Ficken, blasen und andere Delikatessen:

Dirty, Dirtier, and Dirtiest German

As a connoisseur, you have certainly saved this section for last, the *Apfelstrudel*, if you will, of *Talk Dirty: German*. If you have chosen to start the book with this section, you're the kind of person that eats dessert first. In any case, welcome to the dark side of German slang—and oh boy, do those Germans take the *Torte* in this area. More than just widespread sex shops and prostitutes, Germany is known for the raunchiness of its sex industry, namely its porn. Worldwide, it holds a reputation as almost the most perverted nation (second only to Japan, of course). But we won't keep you waiting any longer to get to the good stuff . . . read on . . .

einen Ständer haben

to get a hard-on

Nimm mal deine Hände aus meinen Hosen oder ich krieg sonst 'nen Ständer.

Take your hands out of my pants or I'll get a hard-on.

erschlaffen

to get soft, to go limp

Meine Großmutter lacht darüber, dass mein Großvater ohne Viagra sofort erschlafft.

My grandmother laughs that without Viagra my grandfather immediately goes limp.

feucht werden

to get wet

Hör auf so zu reden, ich bin schon ganz feucht.

Stop talking like that, I'm already all wet.

erregbar

easily aroused

Mein Freund is leicht erregbar.

My boyfriend is easily aroused.

erregen

to excite, to arouse

Nur der Duft deines Tangaslips erregt mich.

Just the smell of your thong panties arouses me.

spitz sein

to be horny; lit. to be pointed or spiky

Schatz, ich bin spitz . . . komm rein inne Kiste.

Sweetie, I'm horny . . . come to bed.

Mösensaft, m.
cunt juice
Robbie liebt es, ihren Mösensaft zu schlecken.
Robbie loves to lap up her cunt juice.

Wermutstropfen, pl.
drops of pre-cum
Als Linda Alans Wermutstropfen erblickte, schrie sie auf und befahl, dass sie sich wieder anziehen.
When Linda saw Alan's drops of pre-cum, she screamed and demanded they both get dressed.

Wonnetropfen, pl.
drops of pre-cum; lit. drops of bliss
Möchtest du mal meine Wonnetropfen auflecken?
Wanna lick my pre-cum?

First Base

abdrücken
to French kiss
Ich hab die zwei in der Disco ganz schön abdrücken sehen.
I saw the two of them French kissing in the disco.

schmusen
to cuddle
Können wir einfach nur schmusen?
Can we just cuddle?

Zungenkuss, m.
French kiss; lit. tongue kiss

Wann hast du deinen ersten Zungenkuss bekommen?
When did you get your first French kiss?

Second Base

Busengrapscher, m.
groper; lit. tit-grabber
Der Typ ist ein alter Busengrapscher.
This guy is a real groper.

gamsig sein
to be aroused, excited
Dieser Film macht mich ganz gamsig.
This movie is making me really excited.

fummeln
second base, petting; lit. to grope
Der Doktor sagt, vom Fummeln allein wird eine Frau nicht schwanger.
The doctor says a girl can't get pregnant just from petting.

The expressions "second base," and "third base" combined are known in German as das Petting. The prelude to "petting" is called Necking in Germany. Yes, the exact same words that were used in English around fifty years ago! Today, you're more likely to "make out" instead. When a German girl isn't ready to "go all the way" yet, she'll suggest "Lass uns nur Petting machen," "Let's just make –out." If you hear this, guys, don't be too disappointed, as you'll still get to touch, lick, and stroke below the belt.

---

jemandem einen blasen

to give someone a blow job

**Selbst für eine Gehaltserhöhung wollte die Sekretärin
ihrem Chef nicht einen blasen.**

*Even for a raise, the secretary didn't want to give her boss a blow
job.*

aussaugen

to blow; lit. to suck out

Guck mal der da. Den würd ich auch mal gern aussaugen!

See the hot guy over there? I'd like to blow him!

Mr. Muschi, m.

Mr. Pussy (from "Sex and the City")

**Mr. Muschi stammt aus der Serie "Sex and the City":
seine ausgefeilte Zungentechnik brachte alle Frauen zum
Höhepunkt.**

*Mr. Pussy comes from the series "Sex and the City": his sophisti-
cated tongue techniques brought all the ladies to climax.*

Blümchensex, m.

boring or standard sex, missionary style; lit. little flower sex

Mit der Angela kannst du nur Blümchensex haben.

With Angela all you get is missionary style.

Ringelpietz mit Anfassen, n.

necking

**Zuerst gab mir Oskar die schärfsten Zungenküsse und
dann blieb's doch nur beim Ringelpietz mit Anfassen.**

*First Oskar started with intense French kissing, but then we never
got beyond that kind of necking.*

Ringelpietz *originally refers to some spontaneous circle dance* (ringel *means round) without form that is often mentioned in children's songs. The idiom* Ringelpiez mit Anfassen *(loop with touching) is used by teenagers for first erotic encounters and erotic party games. It consists of kissing and touching, but no real sex.*

fingern
to finger somebody, to fingerf**k
Jemanden fingern war aufregend, als wir Schüler waren.
In high school it was a great thrill to fingerf**k.

Home Base

Vorspiel, n.
foreplay
Genug Vorspiel, lass uns ernst machen.
Enough foreplay, let's do it.

deflorieren
to deflower
Ich würd gern deine Schwester deflorieren.
I'd love to deflower your sister.

es (mit jemandem) treiben
to f**k
Der Hannes treibt es mit jeder.
Hannes f**ks around.

bumsen
to shag
Jenny, fändest du es ok, wenn ich mit deinem Ex bumsen würde?
Jenny, would it be okay if I shagged your ex?

bollern
to f**k someone's brains out
Du möchtest mich so richtig durchbollern, oder?
You'd like to f**k my brains out, wouldn't you?

knallen
to f**k someone stupid
Du müsstest mal ordentlich von allen Seiten durchgeknallt werden.
You really should be f**ked stupid from all angles.

geigen
to f**k; lit. to fiddle
Hmmm, ich glaub, wir werden uns erst ma' so richtig ordentlich geigen!
Hmmm, I think we'll f**k each other hard.

orgeln
to f**k; lit. to play the organ
Carmen hat sich nach dem ersten date schon orgeln lassen.
Carmen agreed to f**k already after the first date.

nageln
to bone; lit. to nail
Marco sagte, er würde gern die Tanja mal gut und hart nageln wollen.
Marco said he'd like to bone Tanja good and hard.

rammeln

to hump, to be at it; comes from *Ramme*, ram

Sie haben jede Nacht gerammelt wie Kaninchen.

Every night they'd be at it like rabbits.

vögeln

to screw, to bonk; lit. to do like birds, from *Vogel*, bird

Sie haben stundenlang gevögelt.

They screwed each other for hours.

bürsten

to bang; lit. to brush

Alter, du errätst nicht, wen ich gestern gebürstet habe.

Dude, you'll never guess who I banged yesterday.

stupsen

to have tender sex, to make love; lit. to nudge

Na Schatz, sollen wir heute noch ein wenig stupsen?

Sweetie, should we make a little love today?

besorgen

to f**k

Ronni hat's Susi mit seinem harten Fickriemen so richtig besorgt. Susi hat jetzt 'nen Gang wie John Wayne.

Ronnie f**ked Susi with his big hard cock. Now Susi walks like John Wayne.

poppen

to f**k

Du poppst doch alles, was Puls hat.

You'd f**k anything with a pulse.

stöpseln

to f**k; lit. to peg

Mia kann man von vorne und hinten stöpseln. Die macht alles mit.
You can f**k Mia from the front and from behind. She'll go for anything.

ficken
to f**k
Ich hätte Lust, dich jetzt ganz hart zu ficken.
I'd love to f**k you hard.

Natursekt, m.
golden shower; lit. natural bubbly
Stehst du auf Natursekt?
How about a golden shower?
Lit. You dig organic bubbly?

flotter Dreier, m.
ménage à trois, threesome
Hattest du schon mal einen flotten Dreier?
Have you ever had a threesome?

Lümmelgetümmel, n.
group sex, orgy; lit. bugger turmoil
Es gibt gewisse Klubs für Sexspiele. Dort herrscht Lümmelgetümmel.
There are certain clubs for sex games. There you can have an orgy.

Matratzenwunder, n.
woman who is good between the sheets; lit. mattress wonder
Susi ist ein echtes Matratzenwunder.
Susi is really good between the sheets.

kommen

to cum

Oooh Baby, ich möchte die ganze Nacht in dir kommen, du fühlst dich so gut an.

Oooh baby, I want to come in you all night, you feel so good.

abspritzen

to cum; lit. to spray

Komm Baby, lass mich abspritzen.

Come on baby, let me cum.

Soße, f.

cum; lit. sauce

Ich spritze gleich meine Soße ab.

I'm about to cum.

Lit. My sauce is about to run.

Ficksahne, f.

cum; lit. f**k cream

Schau dir das Bettlaken an. Alles voller Ficksahne!

Look at the sheets. All full of cum!

BIBLIOGRAPHY

Androutsopoulos, Jannis K. *Deutsche Jugendsprache*. Frankfurt: Peter Lang, 1998

Ehmann, Hermann. *Endgeil: Das voll korrekte Lexikon der Jugendsprache*. Munich: C. H. Beck, 2005.

Stern, Susan. *These Strange German Ways*. Berlin: Atlantik-Brücke Publication, 1997

Zeidenitz, Stefan and Ben Barkow. *The Xenophobe's Guide to the Germans*. Horsham: Ravette Books, 1996

www.accurapid.com .
www.about.com
www.bbc.co.uk /languages/german
www.coolslang.com
germanslang.wordpress.com
www.goethe.de
www.insultmonger.com
www.mister-wong.de
www.mundmische.de
pukkagerman.com
www.sfs.uni-tuebingen.de
www.spiegel.de/international
www.sprachnudel.de
www.study-in-germany.de
www.urbandictionary.com
www.wikipedia.com
www.wordreference.com
www.wunderland-deutsch.com